The Baptism and Temptation of Christ

A toy glorieux benoit Jhus
et a toy pere de lassus
avec vostre saint esperit
vont anges de grace raemplit
glorieusement marie

Maria — Tunc recedunt angeli ad paradisum et Jhus descendet domum marie, et maria loquitur et dicit sepulcrum [illegible]

Souverain dieu quelle mellodie
mon cueur en est trestout joyeulx
a mon dieu soit la chanteur
de vous sainctz anges glorieux
secret et point mon amoureux
qui me vint icy veoir
se je le puis apparcevoir
de tout bien raemplir mes yeulx

pausa — Certes c'est mon filz gracieux
il fault bien que voyse a luy

Jhus

Valete mere

Marie

Hee mon amy
vous soyes le tresbien venu
et quoy mamour vous aves heu
affaire des que ne vous veux

Jhus

Ouy mere

Marie

C'est bien mon filz
c'est tousjours pour admender
il vous fault ung peu reposser
quar je suy que estes travaillé
et quant vous aves sommeillé
et dormy ung peu sur ce banc
vous aves vostre entendement
mieulx a vostre ayse mon amy

Jhus

Ma mere je vous rans mercy
volantiers je prandre ce bien

Maria

Nous et vous ne ferons plus riens
adieu soyons trestous — explicit

Deo gracias

The last leaf of the manuscript (fol. 17b), containing lines 984–1014, reproduced half-size. (Courtesy Harvard Theatre Collection.)

The Baptism and Temptation of Christ

THE FIRST DAY OF A MEDIEVAL FRENCH PASSION PLAY

EDITED AND TRANSLATED BY
John R. Elliott, Jr.
AND
Graham A. Runnalls

NEW HAVEN AND LONDON
YALE UNIVERSITY PRESS: 1978

Published with assistance from the Kingsley Trust Association Publication Fund established by the Scroll and Key Society of Yale College.

Designed by Thos. Whitridge
and set in Janson type.
Printed in the United States of America by
Vail-Ballou Press, Binghamton, New York.

Published in Great Britain, Europe, Africa, and Asia (except Japan) by Yale University Press, Ltd., London. Distributed in Australia and New Zealand by Book & Film Services, Artarmon, N.S.W., Australia; and in Japan by Harper & Row, Publishers, Tokyo Office.

Library of Congress Cataloging in Publication Data
Main entry under title:

The Baptism and temptation of Christ.

English and French.
Bibliography: p.
1. Jesus Christ—Baptism—Drama. 2. Jesus Christ—Temptation—Drama. I. Elliott, John R. II. Runnalls, Graham A.
PQ1551.B28 842'.3 78-6564
ISBN 0-300-02199-2

Contents

Preface

The Baptism and Temptation of Christ is the title we have given to an untitled manuscript recently discovered in the Harvard Theatre Collection, Cambridge, Massachusetts (MS Thr 262). The manuscript contains the first day of what was probably a seven-day Passion play, the remainder of which is now lost, intended for performance in the north or center of France in the early sixteenth century. The episodes portrayed in our manuscript include the coming of John the Baptist and his early preachings, the Baptism of Christ, and the Temptation by Satan in the desert. This book, which constitutes the first published reference to this text, consists of a detailed study of the play, together with an edition of the French text and a translation into English.

For both historical and literary reasons, *The Baptism and Temptation of Christ* is a text of considerable importance. It represents the first discovery of a hitherto unknown version of a French Passion play for over half a century. Although it is only a single *journée* of a little over a thousand lines, it is particularly significant from the standpoint of literary history, especially with regard to the evolution of Passion plays in France.

The longer Passion play of which our manuscript is a part, which for convenience we shall call *The Harvard Passion*, was almost certainly unrelated to the Gréban-Michel tradition of Passion plays which has appeared to dominate religious dramatic performances in France during the late fifteenth and early sixteenth centuries. The numerous surviving manuscripts of Arnoul Gréban's *Passion* and its later *remaniements*, the printed editions of Jean Michel's *Passion* (itself closely based on Gréban's), as well as the many other late Passion plays which borrowed heavily from them, such as the two *Passions de Valenciennes* of the late 1540s and the so-called *Passion Cyclique* of 1507—all tend to give the impression that the Gréban-Michel tradition was virtually the only one seen on the stage in late medieval France. The *remaniements* of Michel's text that are known to have been performed in the southeastern provinces tend to support this view.

It is now clear, however, that there was at least one other major tradition of Passion plays in France, a tradition preserved mainly by two texts: the present play and the so-called *Passion d'Auvergne*. The latter fragment, though studied briefly by Emile Roy in 1903 and by A. Bossuat in 1944, has been almost completely neglected by recent critics. The main characteristics of this tradition, distinguishing it from the Gréban-Michel tradition, are as follows. The play was divided into several short *journées*, probably seven of them, of between 1500 and 3000 lines each; it started with the John the Baptist episodes and not with Old Testament material; and although the basic action of the play necessarily resembled that of any Passion play and depended on the same biblical, apocryphal, and patristic sources, the treatment of this material was strikingly different from that of the Gréban-Michel texts. In particular, the importance of the role of the Virgin Mary is far greater.

The tradition represented by the *Harvard Passion* and the *Passion d'Auvergne* is probably to be associated with the province of Auvergne. A complete performance of a play in this tradition is known to have taken place at Montferrand in 1477; the *Passion d'Auvergne* shows traces of the Auvergne dialect; and the only other well-known Passion play that bears the slightest resemblance to this tradition is the *Passion de Semur*, which emanates from the neighboring province of Burgundy. Although the present portion of the *Harvard Passion* could well be the work of a northern copyist from the Paris area, its affinities with the Auvergne tradition are unmistakable. The existence of this manuscript thus indicates that in spite of the preponderance of versions of the Gréban-Michel *Passions*, at least one other major tradition was thriving in some parts of France at the end of the Middle Ages.

The manuscript is likewise of considerable interest from a literary point of view. As we have noted, the complete play of which it is a part seems to have consisted of some seven relatively short *journées*, its overall length being therefore much less than that of the Gréban-Michel *Passions*. The result is a greater concision and a reduction in the emphasis placed on sermons and didactic and theological material, with a corresponding increase in the direct dramatization of feelings, particularly those of the Virgin Mary. In *The Baptism and Temptation* each major episode ends with the appearance of Christ's mother. Moreover, a detailed analysis shows that the author (who is nowhere named in the manuscript) has constructed his play in a most thoughtful manner, being especially concerned with questions of balance and structure. For these reasons, it is arguable that the *Baptism and Temptation* is much more approachable for the modern reader than some of the texts in the Gréban-Michel tradition.

In preparing this book we have collaborated closely at all stages. John Elliott is primarily responsible for the translation and for the chapters on the play itself, its staging and its sources. Graham Runnalls transcribed the manuscript and contributed the chapters on the physical characteristics of the manuscript, the language of the play, and its versification. John Elliott was responsible for the initial discovery of the manuscript and for the early detective work.

We wish to thank Jeanne T. Newlin, Curator of the Harvard Theatre Collection, for her help and encouragement in planning this edition, and Donald Maddox, who assisted in the initial examination of the manuscript. We are grateful to the directors of the Houghton Library, Harvard College, for permission to publish the manuscript.

John R. Elliott, Jr.
Graham A. Runnalls

Introduction

1 The Manuscript

1.1 *History and discovery*

1.1.1 The existence of MS Thr 262, belonging to the Harvard Theatre Collection, Cambridge, Massachusetts, was brought to the attention of John Elliott in 1972 by the curator, Jeanne T. Newlin. The manuscript had been purchased by the Theatre Collection in 1946 from the New York office of Pierre Berès, a Paris book dealer, but remained uncatalogued until 1970. On two occasions, in 1969 and 1971, it was placed on exhibit in Cambridge for meetings of learned societies, but it received no scholarly examination until Professor Elliott's researches initiated the present edition.

1.1.2 Ownership of the manuscript before 1946 has not been definitely determined. Two documents preserved with the manuscript suggest that one of its nineteenth-century owners misidentified its contents, which would account for the lack of attention it has received until now. The documents also suggest that the manuscript was in private hands throughout at least part of the nineteenth century and probably until its sale around the time of World War II.

The first and more important of these documents is an autograph letter bound in with the manuscript. It is dated 9 March 1875 and signed "P. Paris." The text reads:

Cher Monsieur,

Si votre manuscrit s'arrête après *la tentation de N.S.* comme vous me le marquez, il ne contient que les onze ou douze premières scènes de la Première Journée du grand *Mystère de*

> *la Passion*, soit revu par Jean Michel, soit avant cette révision. Si vous pouvez consulter le sixième volume de mon histoire des *Manuscrits françois de la Bibliothèque* aujourd'hui *Nationale*, (en attendant qu'elle redevienne *Royale*,) et surtout *Les Toiles peintes et Tapisseries de Reims* in '4° de mon frère Louis Paris, vous y reconnoîtrez l'analyse de votre manuscrit, qui pour n'être pas complet a pourtant une assez grande valeur.

The author of this letter was Paulin Paris, an antiquarian and bibliographer, who was evidently consulted about the manuscript by its owner. The owner's name, unfortunately, does not appear in Paris's salutation. It is clear from the wording of the letter that Paris did not actually see the manuscript itself. His guess that the text of the play it contained was a *remaniement* of the Arnoul Gréban-Jean Michel *Passion* appears to have been based on a summary of the subject-matter of the play furnished by the owner. None of the works to which Paris refers contains any information on the manuscript, nor does the play itself bear any resemblance, verbal or narrative, to the Gréban-Michel *Passion* (see below, 3.6.1). Nevertheless, the owner appears to have been satisfied with Paris's "identification" and to have taken no further steps to have the manuscript studied by experts. Instead, he proceeded to have it bound, along with the "identifying" letter from Paris, which had been tipped in, with the title *Mystère du XVe Siècle* stamped on the spine. This title is also written, in a nineteenth-century hand, on the back of the first leaf of the Manuscript. As the binding is a typical late nineteenth-century binding, we may guess that this happened soon after the receipt of Paris's letter in 1875.

The second document reveals that Paris's misidentification of the manuscript remained the only attempt to study the work before its sale to the Harvard Theatre Collection. A letter to Professor William Van Lennep of Harvard from Mr. Lucien Goldschmidt of the New York office of Pierre Berès, dated 23 October 1946, offers the manuscript for sale under the title *Le Grand Mystère de la Passion*, that is, the title of Gréban's *Passion* erroneously applied to the work by Paris.

The Berès letter also copies other phrases from Paris's description, while offering no new information. We may conclude from this that the manuscript remained in private hands from 1875 to 1946, possibly as part of a large collection that was kept intact until the latter date.

1.1.3 There is little information to guide us in identifying the owner or owners of the manuscript either before or during this period. A brief reference to a manuscript which might possibly be the one under discussion is made in a study of fragments of medieval *mystères* that appeared in *Romania* in 1890. The author, E. Picot, mentions "un fragment, conservé dans un manuscrit qui nous appartient, d'un mystère assez peu developpé." The fragment, he goes on, "comprend la première journée tout entière." Picot gives no further details as to the contents or length of this manuscript, nor did he ever see fit to publish it. The fact that Picot's library was purchased by Pierre Berès in 1935, however, leads us to suppose that the manuscript referred to by Picot may have been identical with the one we present here, in which case he must have acquired it sometime between 1875 and 1890. We have been unable to find documentary evidence of such a purchase, though, nor have we found any further mention of the manuscript in scholarly writings, by Picot or anyone else, in this or the previous century. Mr. Goldschmidt has confirmed to the present editors that he received the manuscript for sale in the United States directly from M. Berès, whose records show no trace of its origins but who has suggested to us its possible provenance among Picot's papers. Of the ownership of the manuscript prior to 1875 there appears to be no surviving information.

1.2 *Description of the manuscript*

1.2.1 The MS consists of seventeen folios of paper, measuring approximately 28 cm. by 19 cm. The first folio recto contains the Incipit and the names and descriptions of two major characters in the play, God the Father and John the Baptist. The rest of the recto and the whole of the verso of fol. 1 are blank, with the exception of the phrase "Un mystère du xv siècle," written in a nineteenth-century hand at the top left-hand corner of the verso. Portions of the phrase are badly smudged and the whole is nearly invisible due to the heavy backing-paper onto which this leaf has been pasted. The remaining sixteen folios contain the surviving text of just over 1000 lines of dialogue, together with the names of the speakers and some stage directions. Each of these folios has one column of text on the recto and one on the verso. The first line of text on fol. 2 recto appears to be the beginning of the play; the last lines of fol. 17 verso are clearly the end of a *journée.* There is probably a lacuna of one or more folios between folios 2 and 3.

Folio 1 is badly torn; folio 2 is more heavily worn than the following leaves, and some of its edges have been torn. The remaining leaves have no tears and have worn about equally, including the last, fol. 17. This degree of wearing supports the view that fol. 2 represents the start of the play; moreover, it suggests that fol. 17, even if it is the end of a *journée*, is certainly not the end of the whole play. Indeed, it is probable that for most of its history since the sixteenth century the MS contained further sections of the play following fol. 17, and that these were separated from the rest of the MS at a relatively recent date. We have not, however, been able to trace any such missing sections.

The present binding of the MS, dating from the late nineteenth century, is of board cased in brown leather, with the title *Mystère du XVe siècle* stamped in gold on the spine. The letter from Paulin Paris, written in 1875 (see above, 1.1.2), is tipped in with the text. There is no bookplate, coat of arms, or ornament betraying the name of the owner of the MS. For the binding, the inner edge of each leaf has been pasted onto a strip of thin paper; fol. 1, however, has been completely pasted onto a whole sheet of much heavier paper.

1.2.2 *Watermarks.* Only one watermark appears, on about half of the 17 folios; it is a "fleur de lis simple posée dans un écu couronné," from which hangs a "moucheture d'hermine," to use the description of Briquet.[1] Briquet's reference work on watermarks contains a large family of such marks, all of French origin. Our own mark is very close to, but not iden-

1. C. M. Briquet, *Les Filigranes,* ed. A. Stevenson, 4 vols.

tical with, Briquet's example no. 7196; it also has many points in common with no. 7175. It is, of course, unwise to treat watermarks as infallible guides to dating texts, but, used with caution, they can help establish approximate dates and support other forms of dating evidence.[2] Briquet's no. 7196 is accompanied by the following notes: "7196. 29.5 x 41. Fresne l'Archevêque 1494 (A. Loire-Inférieure); Var. id. Grenoble 1495; Bretagne 1496; Namur 1546." His example no. 7175, dated 1551, is located at Tours. Nearly all the family of related marks date from the first half of the sixteenth century. A reasonable, conservative conclusion would be that our text was written in the first half of the sixteenth century.

1.2.3 *Scribes.* The MS, as it stands at present, appears to be the work of three different scribes, whom we shall label A, B, and C. They may be differentiated not only by handwriting but also by ink color. A is by far the most important; the whole of the text, all the names of the characters, the Incipit, and most of the stage directions are his work. B has contributed some further stage directions (in brackets in the edition). C, a much more modern hand than A or B (probably added in the eighteenth or nineteenth century), is responsible for some lines in the left-hand margins and for a few more quite unnecessary stage directions.[3] For example, C adds the words *lui répond* to A's *Satan* (639) and *dit à Satan* to A's *Asmo* (647). Since C's contribution is clearly a much later superfluous addition, and is in no way part of the original text, we have omitted his work from the edition.

The handwriting of Scribe A is a clear and carefully written cursive, characteristic of the late fifteenth and early sixteenth centuries; it manifests considerable similarities to examples from this period given in Prou and in Lieftinck.[4] The most

2. See A. Stevenson's remarks, pp. *31–*34, in his introduction to Briquet, *Les Filigranes*, vol. 1: "It is a mistake to suppose that watermarks are keys to precise dates, and yet more often than has been supposed, they offer clues to approximate ones."

3. Stage directions after lines 308, 627, 639, 647, 808, 852, 972.

4. M. Prou, *Recueil de fac-similés;* cf. pl. 38, a *quittance* from Sens, dated 1475. G. I. Lieftinck, *Manuscrits datés conservés dans les Pays-Bas;* cf. pl. 251, dated 1500–04.

striking individual feature of A's hand is his digraph for the palatal *l*, which consists of a normal *l* followed by an *l* with a tail like that of a *j*. Other details about his spelling and handwriting appear respectively in the chapters on the language of the text and on editorial principles.

By examining closely the size and spacing of A's writing, one can see how he went about copying the text. The first stage consisted of copying simply the dialogue and the names of the speakers, with no stage directions except at two major breaks in the action, what one might now call changes of scene, where he wrote in *Pausa cum silete.*[5] At the second stage, A went through the text adding further stage directions, some in Latin, some in French, usually in smaller handwriting. These directions were introduced, at the appropriate place, in either the left- or right-hand margins, and this positioning in the margins has been reflected in our edition. The additions were written in small neat handwriting and were carefully underlined.

Scribe B's hand, though similar to and approximately contemporary with A's, is more cursive and florid, showing signs of rapid and careless execution. The underlining is freer and more spontaneous. Moreover, B's ink appears to have faded more than A's. B's contribution consists of about fourteen additional stage directions, all but one in Latin, spread over the first seven folios only.[6] Most of these additions are quite unexceptionable, but two call for comment. In the first instance, B wishes one particular effect to occur earlier than A originally intended: during the scene of Jesus's baptism by John, B wants the symbolic dove to descend after line 290, whereas A indicates this effect after line 300. The result is that the MS now contains two stage directions for the same effect.

The second of B's stage directions worthy of note occurs after line 66: *C'est assavoir Andrieu, Natanael, Nazon et saint Samuel.* This is not so much a new stage direction as an explana-

5. See the stage directions after lines 564 and 844.

6. See the stage directions after lines 40, 55, 66, 82, 184, 190, 232, 234, 290, 336, 346.

tory note, clarifying A's stage direction: *Tunc expolient se illi iiij^{or}*. As the MS stands at present, there is no way of knowing, on reaching line 66, who *illi iiij^{or}* are; this is because of a lacuna after fol. 2. Several factors indicate that some of the original play has been lost between line 60, the last of fol. 2, and line 61, the first of fol. 3: the change in the rhyme scheme and scansion, the interruption of John's prayer, the sudden appearance of new characters, the absence of material that would normally be found in the John the Baptist episodes, etc.[7] As a result of this lacuna, only two of the four men whom John prepares to baptize at line 67 have already appeared, Samuel and Saint Andrieu. B's addition is therefore extremely useful, as it provides the names of the two others as well, Nathanael and Nason, information which is gleaned from the rest of the scene.[8]

It is therefore clear that B's work on the MS took place after the loss of the folio(s) in question. Given that B's handwriting is roughly contemporaneous with A's (first half of the sixteenth century), one can conclude that this loss occurred at a very early stage in the history of the MS.

7. For a fuller discussion of the lacuna, see below, 2.1.3.

8. In this explanatory note Scribe B has inadvertently canonised Samuel. Elsewhere in the text, the name Samuel is not preceded by the title "Saint."

2 The Play

2.1 *Contents*

2.1.1 *The Baptism and Temptation of Christ* dramatizes two episodes in the life of Jesus, combined to form a single play. The episodes are The Baptism of Jesus and The Temptation in the Wilderness. Each episode is divided into several "scenes," which may be enumerated as follows:

I. The Baptism (1–564)

(1) (1–60) In the Desert, God the Father commands Saint John the Baptist to preach his word and baptize the people.

(2) (61–100) John goes to the river Jordan, preaches, and baptizes four disciples: Samuel, Andrew, Nathanael, and Nason.

(3) (101–234) John goes to Bethany to preach. Pharisees and noblemen, including Joseph of Arimathaea, come to hear him and are converted. He leads them to the Jordan to be baptized.

(4) (235–402) In Nazareth, Jesus says farewell to his mother, Mary, and goes to the Jordan to be baptized by John. Mary prays for his safe return. Jesus baptizes John after his own baptism, then goes to the Desert to fast for forty days.

(5) (403–482) In his palace, Herod consults the Jewish priests about John, listens to prophecies read from the Scriptures, and determines to find out who John is.

(6) (483–564) Herod's messengers—Malifferas, Natort, and Berith—go to the Jordan to interrogate John and take his

answers back to their master. Herod decides to send for John.

II. The Temptation (565–1014)

(7) (565–699) The Council in Hell: Lucifer, having heard of the Baptism, consults the devils about Jesus and decides to send Satan and Asmo to tempt him.

(8) (700–844) In the Desert, the devils tempt Jesus three times and are rebuffed.

(9) (845–1014) God sends his angels to comfort Mary, to minister to Jesus, and to lead him back to Nazareth to be reunited with his mother.

2.1.2 According to the initial rubric, these episodes comprise the first day (*premier dimanche*) of a longer Passion play. That *premier dimanche* (literally "first Sunday") in fact means the first *journée* of the play is suggested by the following evidence: (a) the Baptism was a common starting-point for French Passion plays, as, for example, in the Jean Michel *Passion* of 1486, where the episode occupies lines 889–3339, the first 888 lines consisting of a prologue; (b) the occurrence of the phrase *premier dimanche*, as well as *second dimanche*, *dimanche tiers*, and *quart dimanche*, in 1477 in the municipal records of the city of Montferrand in the Auvergne—the probable locale of the play from which our play has been derived (see below, 2.1.4)—with reference to the payment of minstrels for their work in a performance of the *Passion d'Auvergne*, the first four *journées* of which evidently took place on Sundays.[1]

The manuscript also contains abundant evidence that our play is, with the exception of some sixty to one hundred lines, the *complete* first day of the Passion sequence to which it once belonged. The opening lines of dialogue comprise an invitation from the Archangel Raphael to the audience to "begin" the day's festivities with a song:

> Or conmancés, mes conpaignons;
> Feisons a noustre Dieu joyeux rondel.

1. A. Bossuat, "Une représentation de la Passion à Montferrand en 1477," pp. 336–39.

Now begin, my friends;
Let us sing a joyful rondeau to our Lord.

And at the end of the text contained in the manuscript the scribe has written *Explicit*, together with a propitiatory *Deo gracias* (1014).

2.1.3 *Lacunae.* The absence of one or possibly two leaves is evident between folios 2b and 3a of our text (see above, 1.2.3). These must originally have contained the end of "Scene 1" and the beginning of "Scene 2," comprising John the Baptist's journey from the Desert to the Jordan; the entrance of the four disciples, Andrew, Nathanael, Nason, and Samuel; their conversion by John and his "instructions" (62) to them on baptism; John's denunciation of Herodias (118); and his preaching of two sermons mentioned later in the text, *Parate vias* (121) and *Faictes trestous penictence* (122). The substance of the sermons may be reconstructed from the biblical accounts (Luke 3 : 19; Luke 3 : 4; Matthew 3 : 2), as well as from the parallel scenes in the *Passion de Semur* (lines 3429–62) and the Jean Michel *Passion* (1548–800).

The total number of lines in our manuscript in its original state thus probably numbered between 1100 and 1150 (the 1014 lines of the present text plus one or two leaves averaging 60 lines each). While this total makes *The Baptism and Temptation* considerably shorter than the average *journée* of most fifteenth-century Passions (10,000 lines for the first day of the Gréban *Passion*, 6,000 for Jean Michel, 4,000 for *Semur*), it is in keeping with what we know about the length of most sixteenth-century multi-day religious plays, thus tending to confirm the physical evidence of the manuscript dating it in the first half of the sixteenth century. The average length of the *Valenciennes Passion* of 1547, for example, is 2,000 lines per day.[2] The series of four biblical plays published by Marguerite de Navarre in 1547 average 1300 lines each, while the series of twelve *Mystères de Notre Dame de Liesse* written by Jean Louvet and performed in Paris between 1536 and 1550

2. E. Konigson, *La représentation d'un mystère de la Passion à Valenciennes en 1547*.

range in length from 800 to 1800 lines apiece.[3] The Passion which our play initiates was thus probably conceived on a considerably more economical scale than the earlier Passions in the Gréban-Michel tradition.

2.1.4 *The "Harvard Passion" and the "Passion d'Auvergne."* The evidence of two manuscript fragments of the *Passion d'Auvergne* in the Bibliothèque Nationale gives us further reason to dissociate the present play from the Gréban-Michel tradition and permits us to speculate with some confidence on the contents of the longer play of which it was once a part. These fragments are preserved in MS BN Nouvelle Acquisition Française 462 and contain parts of two *journées* of a Passion play written in the French of the Auvergne region of central France.[4] Watermarks date the fragments from the period 1460–80. Fragment A (1900 lines) contains the beheading of John the Baptist and the public life of Jesus up to the conversion of Mary Magdalene. Fragment B (2700 lines) contains the Passion story proper from the Judgment of Pilate through the Crucifixion and Burial of Jesus. Numerous similarities in style, versification, and the names of characters suggest that the present manuscript is probably a *remaniement* of the now lost first day of the *Passion d'Auvergne.*

The resemblances between the two manuscripts may be summarized as follows. Characters such as Zeras, Lazay, Finees, Malifferas, and Asmo, not to be found in any other French Passion play, appear in precisely the same roles in the *Passion d'Auvergne.* The devils are given "lettres procuratoires," as at line 672 of our play, and speak in *triolets,* as at lines 71–78, 361–68, 662–69, 682–89, and 861–68. A stage direction has the angels sing a song, *Glorieuse Marie,* the full text of which is given in our play (974–88). Curious spellings in our manuscript occasionally reflect the dialect of the Auvergne play: *Bourgonnhe* (811), *mignhons* (898), and the digraph used by

3. L. Petit de Julleville, *Les mystères,* 2 : 608–25.

4. For a detailed description of the *Passion d'Auvergne* manuscript and excerpts from its text, see E. Roy, *Le mystère de la Passion en France,* 2 : 359–77. Some errors of transcription by Roy have been silently corrected in the present discussion.

scribe A to represent palatal *l* (see 1.2.3 and 6.2b) may have its origin in the Auvergne scribe's use of *lh* for the same sound. Above all, the emphasis in the two plays on the role of the Virgin Mary links them together: each of the two Auvergne fragments ends with a Mary scene, as does our play. In short, nearly all the features that make our play otherwise unique among French Passion plays may also be found in the Auvergne fragments.

2.1.5 *The longer play.* With the help of the Auvergne fragments and of the municipal records of Montferrand which record a performance of that play, or a very similar one, in 1477,[5] we may now attempt to reconstruct the longer Passion play of which our manuscript originally formed the first part. We may note, to begin with, what appears to be a direct reference in our text to the contents of Fragment A of the *Passion d'Auvergne.* At the end of "Scene 5" of our play Herod, after consulting the Jewish priests about John the Baptist, decides to send for him:

> Or sa, il le me fault ouÿr
> Unne fois en toute ma vie.
>
> Well, then, I must hear him
> At least once in my life.
> [563–64]

As this meeting does not occur in our *journée*, we may assume that it was to be a feature of a future day's entertainment. The Auvergne Fragment A provides us with just such an episode, an extended series of scenes depicting Herod's feast and the dance of Salome; the "temptation" of Herod, Herodias, and Salome by Satan, Beelzebub, and Asmo; the beheading of John by Malifferas; and the delivery of John's soul to Limbo by the Archangel Gabriel. It is more than likely, then, that Fragment A of the *Passion d'Auvergne* gives us at least part of the contents that were intended for a day that followed soon after our *journée*.

5. Bossuat, "Une représentation de la Passion."

That Fragment A represents the third and not the second *journée* of the play is indicated by a stage direction on fol. 15^r, misinterpreted by Roy, directing that some music be sung "sicut in secunda dominica," that is, just as on the second Sunday. A similar rubric on fol. 34^r orders Jesus to say grace just as he had at the marriage at Cana. Between Fragment A and Fragment B at least one further *journée* must have taken place, containing the Entry to Jerusalem and the Trial of Jesus. Fragment B, which depicts the Crucifixion, was thus the fifth *journée* of the play, and the Montferrand records refer to at least two other days, probably completing the drama: "le mistere de la Resurrection" and "le mistere derrenier [i.e. dernier] de l'Ascension."[6]

If we are correct in linking the *Harvard Passion* and the *Passion d'Auvergne* to the Montferrand production, we may conclude that our manuscript preserves the first day of a longer Passion play that contained at least seven *journées* dramatizing the ministry, death, and resurrection of Jesus. Analysis of the Montferrand records separately from the manuscript texts verifies that at least seven *journées* were involved, though we cannot be sure that there were not more. Nor can we assign exact dates of performance to most of these *journées*, other than noting that all of them appear to have been played on Sundays, with the single exception of "le mistere du lundi de la Pentecoste" ("the mystery of Pentecost Monday," i.e. Whitmonday). In 1477 Whitmonday occurred on May 26. Though no subject is given for that day, the records do tell us that the Entry to Jerusalem was played on May 4. As that was the fourth day of the play, according to our best calculations, we may probably assume that the play began on a Sunday soon after Easter (April 6) and concluded with the Ascension on Whitmonday.

2.2 *Structure*

2.2.1 In calling the divisions of our play "scenes" we must be careful not to think of the word in its modern sense, for the

6. Ibid., pp. 341, 343–44.

author's characteristic structural technique is *entrelacement*, the linking together of episodes into a continuous, uninterrupted whole. Characters commonly speak to one another as they move from one location to another; the movement of single characters is typically "covered" by the speech of a different character in a different location; and in some cases two "scenes" may actually be performed simultaneously. We may cite as an example of the first method the conversation between Malifferas and Berith as they journey from the Jordan to Herod's Palace (537–46); of the second, Mary's prayer as Jesus moves from Nazareth to the Jordan (259–70); and of the third, Jesus's monologue in Nazareth in the midst of John's baptizing of the Pharisees (191–226). This reliance on simultaneous, interlocking action is characteristic of the structural technique of French Passion plays in general and contrasts sharply with the simple juxtaposition of scenes in such English mystery cycles as the York, Wakefield, and Chester plays (but not the N-Town and the Cornish cycles, which show French influence).[7]

In addition to interweaving the individual scenes of his play, our author has carefully constructed parallels and contrasts between the two larger halves of the work in order to link them together into a unified whole. The Baptism is presented as a preparation of Jesus for his public life, a purification before doing battle with the devil. God's call to John the Baptist to start his mission at the beginning of the Baptism episode is complemented by the formal "commissioning" of Asmo and Satan by Lucifer for their contrasting task at the beginning of the Temptation episode. Herod's consultation with Jewish priests about what to do with John is paralleled by Lucifer's consultation with his fellow-devils about what to do with Jesus. Above all, the relationship between Jesus and Mary bridges both halves of the play and stands as the central focus of the drama. Before leaving on his mission, Jesus goes to his mother to tell her of his choice and to bid her farewell (235–40). Mary is saddened and begs him to stay longer with

7. See O. Jodogne, "La structure des mystères français."

her, but she finally accepts his decision, praying to God that he may return safely (242–70). When Jesus has completed his baptism, his fasting, and his struggle with Satan, Mary prays that he may be given some of the "supper" that she has prepared for him (851). Jesus also asks for the "supper" (925). God the Father then sends his angels to comfort Mary, to bring the "supper" to Jesus, and finally to return him to Nazareth to "gladden" his mother (967) and rest from his labors (1005). Literary analysis thus confirms the physical evidence of the manuscript itself as to the unity of the first *journée* of the *Harvard Passion*.

2.3 *Staging*

2.3.1 *The Baptism and Temptation* is written for the usual "mansion and place" staging of medieval religious plays, that is, for a series of scaffolds or "mansions" representing specific locales, arranged about a central unlocalized playing-area or "place." Five principal scaffolds are indicated in the play:

Heaven
Mary's home in Nazareth
Herod's palace
the Temple (of the High Priests, Annas and Caiaphas)
Hell

In addition, there was possibly also a separate scaffold for musicians, though this is not specified in the text (see below, 2.3.4). Four other locales, probably represented by scenic emblems and arranged in the "place," are required for the action:

the Jordan River
Bethany (indicated as being near the Jordan)
the Desert
the Mountain

As no staging diagram is included in the manuscript, we cannot tell whether the playing-area was circular, as in Jean

Fouquet's famous miniature *The Martyrdom of Saint Apollonia*[8] or rectangular, as depicted in the frontispiece of the manuscript of the *Valenciennes Passion* of 1547.[9] If we assume performance in front of a church, as at Montferrand for the *Passion d'Auvergne*, the latter is perhaps more probable. The the audience was close to the action and probably surrounded it on at least three sides is indicated by the number of times they are addressed directly by the actors and occasionally invited to join in the singing of hymns (1–8, 301–06, 425, 724–25, 1013–14.

Details of the scenic structures required in the play may be gleaned from the text itself, from comparison with other plays, and from the Montferrand records which document the expenses for the production of the *Passion d'Auvergne* in 1477. The five principal scaffolds are identical in the locales they represent to those depicted in the Valenciennes drawing, with the exception of Limbo, which is not called for in this *journée* but which is used in Fragment A of the *Passion d'Auvergne*. They may therefore have been similarly constructed. (On April 11 an expenditure was recorded for "deux douzenes de potz . . . a fere les limbes dans yfer.") Wires for flying the angels from the Heaven scaffold to other scaffolds and to the "place" may have been used, as they were at Valenciennes. Such flights are indicated at lines 310, 346, 868, 903, 973, and 988. "White doves/ Flying down from the sky," are seen by Saint John (334–35) and indicated by stage directions at 290 and 310. The Jordan River may have been constructed, as was *la mer* at Valenciennes, out of dried, stretched sheepskins painted blue. It would appear that the Jordan was shaped more like a lake or a sea than a river, as John and his disciples are said to go "around Jordan to Bethany" (97 SD). There was no need for the river to contain water, as the baptism was probably accomplished with water kept in a vial, as in the contemporary baptismal service (see note to line 232). The Desert was probably, as at Montferrand, symbolized by a few trees,

8. See Fouquet, *The Hours of Etienne Chevalier*, ed. Cl. Schaefer, p. 45.
9. See B. Gascoigne, *World Theatre: An Illustrated History*, pl. 10.

cut down for that purpose and placed in the playing area ("du boys de quoy a esté fait le desert pour jouer la Passion."[10] Hell was undoubtedly the traditional monster's jaws, gaping wide to receive the souls of sinners and threatening to impale them on its sharp teeth (see lines 835–36). At Montferrand, the Hell-Mouth was also covered with thorns.[11] The devils' references to "taut chains" (590), "boiling cauldrons" (691), and the "tooth of Cerberus" (835) may all indicate actual stage properties—the boiling cauldron and the teeth may be plainly seen in the Valenciennes frontispiece. The same is probably true of the ubiquitous mentions of Hell's fire: Montferrand expended a large sum of money for "xiii livres de podre de canon pour la Passion."[12]

2.3.2 *Costumes.* In his unfinished list of *dramatis personae* Scribe A tells us in detail of the costumes of two of the chief characters, God the Father and John the Baptist. The costuming of several others may be inferred from the text and the stage directions. God the Father is described as bearded, wearing a hooded cloak and a papal tiara, and holding a sceptre. Evidently he did not wear a mask. Saint John appears according to his biblical description, bearded and dressed in a camelskin, and is further described as

> Hairy as a calf,
> Clothed in a very crude robe
> Which he wears like a sack,
> Almost naked, lean as a bear.
> [555–58]

The four disciples are dressed in simple garments, presumably medieval rather than biblical in style, which they remove to be baptized. The two noblemen and two Pharisees are dressed more expensively, but they too remove their clothes for baptism. No indication of costuming is given in the text for Jesus,

10. Bossuat, "Une représentation de la Passion," p. 336. For the Limbo reference, see p. 337.
11. Ibid., pp. 335–36.
12. Ibid., p. 336.

Mary (who, according to the Montferrand records, was played by a boy), the angels, or the devils, with the exception of Satan. Satan disguises himself as a hermit for the first temptation (699 SD), as a priest for the second (754 SD), and as a king for the third (808 SD). He carries Jesus to the top of the Temple on his shoulders (746 SD) and to the top of the Mountain in the hood of his cloak (793–95).

2.3.3 *Acting*. The stage directions which the two scribes have seen fit to furnish, while not numerous, give us some insight into the style, or styles, of acting that they imagined as fitting for the play. Leaving aside those directions which simply indicate a character's speaking or listening (e.g., 100, 129), and those which have to do solely with movement from one place to another (e.g., 97, 106), we find that of the ones remaining a little less than half (fifteen) have to do with music and the remainder (eighteen) with actions which we may call symbolic or ceremonial. The ceremonial directions include kneeling and rising, either for blessing or in prayer (10, 40, 55, 190, 336, 699); the disrobing and rerobing of candidates for baptism (66, 82, 190, 290, 300, 346, 368); the pouring of baptismal water (78, 233, 293); the descent of the dove (290, 310); the donning of disguise (699, 754, 808); the presentation of offerings (862, 868); the eating of sanctified food (951, 954, 959). These symbolic actions, together with the frequent use of liturgical music (see 2.3.4, below), suggest a measured, formal acting style befitting the sacramental subject of the play. This style, however, must be juxtaposed with the blunt, irreverent language and behavior of the devil-scenes, which parody and blaspheme against "sacred" manners. Yet a third style, retaining some of the dignity of the ceremonial scenes but adding a heightened emotional realism to it, is characteristic of the exchanges between Jesus and Mary, as well as of their monologues and prayers. (The fact that Mary was probably played by a boy did not deter the author from writing intense pathos into her part.) The result is a frequent alternation of moods, resembling a series of musical movements.

2.3.4 *Music*. Either vocal or instrumental music is indicated as being performed at least fifteen times during the course of the play, possibly more often if the frequent stage direction *pausa* is accepted as a musical term. Vocal music is sung exclusively by the angels and is designated by such terms as *rondel* and *cantus*. At the beginning of the play, the angels sing, probably with the audience, a *joyeux rondel*, *Concinamus nato Emanuel* (1–2). In the scene of the Baptism, the angels descend with the dove and sing two stanzas of a *dulci cantu* in praise of the Savior, repeating the hymn as they ascend at the end of the scene (311–26, 346). After Christ's victory over Satan, the angels again descend, bringing heavenly bread, and lead the audience in singing a hymn, *Du pain de gloire*, in its praise (869–72). Finally, as they bring Jesus from the Desert home to Nazareth, they sing a song of praise in honor of Mary, *Glorieuse Marie*, of which three stanzas are given in the text (974–88). In addition, the rubric *Tunc judicamur* (236), occurring in the margin of the manuscript at the point when John pours the baptismal water over Nicodemus, is possibly the title of a hymn to be sung by the other disciples or by the angelic choir.

Instrumental music is signaled by such terms as *silete*, *pausa cum silete*, and perhaps by *pausa* alone. The various terms have been defined by Howard Mayer Brown as follows: "A *silete* is a piece of music used to quiet the spectators, whereas a *pausa* is any musical interlude." Brown adds, however, that "the exact nature of these instrumental interludes is nowhere clearly stated."[13] Flourishes, played by an instrumental consort, are clearly indicated at lines 101, 191, and 234 by the term *silete* as a means of introducing new characters to the play and/or signaling the end of a scene. The phrase *pausa cum silete* occurs six times, four times at the end of a scene (402, 564, 699, 844) and twice in the middle (66, 82). Both instances of the latter occur in "Scene 2," where the interludes "cover" the disrobing and rerobing of the disciples for baptism. The term *pausa* used alone is by far the most frequent of the stage directions in our play, occurring eighteen times, and the most difficult to interpret. Occasionally, it appears to be synonymous with *silete*, as at 290 and 351 where the rerobing of Jesus and the undress-

13. *Music in the French Secular Theatre, 1400–1550*, p. 47.

ing of John for baptism would seem to call for the same "covering" music that was earlier indicated by *silete* at lines 66 and 82, as well as at 368 and 923, where the term coincides with the end of a scene. At other times, however, *pausa* occurs in contexts where music would seem distinctly out of place and silence more natural. The nine instances in the play where this takes place are:

273: the *pausa* separates Jesus's words to the audience from his greeting to John the Baptist.
306: separating God's words to the audience from his orders to the angels to "descend" to Jesus.
425: separating Malifferas's remark to the audience that he is out of breath from his formal greeting to Herod.
536: separating Berith's farewell to John from his instructions to his fellow emissaries.
538: separating Malifferas's remark that he is "thirsty" from his request to his companions to push on toward Herod—a "pause" that may have included a good deal of improvised comic business and perhaps dialogue.
876: separating Mary's greeting to the angels from her questioning of them as to what has happened to her son.
951: the *pausa* here allows time for Jesus's eating of the heavenly bread—the scribe indicates that it is to be a *modica pausa*.
997: separating Mary's exclamations of surprise at the angelic melody from her recognition that Jesus has returned with them.

In all these instances the term *pausa* would seem to indicate a silence, allowing for business or movement or simply a change of mood. If our manuscript was intended to serve as a prompt copy, the direction *pausa* may be solely for the benefit of the prompter, to prevent early warnings. Because the meaning of all these terms is in dispute, however, they have been left in their original Latin forms in the translation.

It seems clear, then, that music would have played an important part in any production of our play. Brown has shown that the normal composition of the instrumental consort for such plays included trumpets, drums, organs, pipes, and other wind instruments, and that the vocal music consisted of both plainchant and polyphony. The Fouquet miniature shows three slide trumpets, two cornets, and a bagpipe in use for the scene of the Martyrdom of Saint Apollonia. The Montferrand records document payments to five *menestriers* and give the names of two organists, several trumpeters, and one player of a *barbarat taborin* (a metal drum), all of whom were employed in the performance of the *Passion d'Auvergne*.[14] The frequency with which music is called for in our play lends support to the conjecture that a separate scaffold may have been erected for the musicians' use, like that shown by Fouquet.

14. Bossuat, "Une représentation de la Passion," pp. 338–39.

3 Sources

3.1 *The Baptism and Temptation* is an "original" play, within the meaning of that term applicable to medieval religious drama. Several of the incidents that it dramatizes are unique, occurring nowhere else in the surviving drama of the Middle Ages, though all may be traced ultimately to written sources. In its more conventional scenes the play is best described as an original blend of traditional materials. Though it shares these scenes with other Passion plays, it copies none of them and succeeds in producing its own characteristic dramatic effect.

The particular effect for which the author of our play appears to strive is to heighten his audience's awareness of the human meaning of the Gospel narratives. To that end he draws on a wide variety of scriptural, literary, and theological sources, combining them in such a way as to emphasize the humanity of Christ, the reality of his sufferings, and the emotional bond between Christ and his mother, the Virgin Mary. The latter emphasis is perhaps the most unique element in the play, surpassing the Marian focus of even the Jean Michel *Passion*. The author's most important sources, aside from the Bible, are two meditative Lives of Christ which had already brought similar emphases to their literary treatment of the subject—the *Meditationes vitae Christi* attributed to Saint Bonaventure (c. 1275) and the *Vita Christi* of Ludolphus de Saxonia (c. 1375). A large number of other post-biblical sources, however, also contribute to the play, ranging from the apocryphal gospels to other religious plays of the period. For convenience we may divide the sources of *The Baptism and Temptation* into five classes:

Canonical Scriptures
Apocryphal Gospels
Writings of the Church Fathers
Meditative Lives of Christ
Other Plays and Theatrical Traditions

Throughout the following discussion the reader should bear in mind that much of the material furnished by these sources is repeated over and over again in the literature of the Middle Ages. We have sought here to identify only the earliest or best-known versions containing the material drawn on in the play. Intermediate sources may well have existed, however, by which this material actually found its way into the hands of the author.

3.2 *Canonical Scriptures*

3.2.1 The basic account of the Baptism and the Temptation is, of course, to be found in the New Testament. Our text refers to all four of the Evangelists, showing particular preference for Matthew and Luke (Mark does not describe the Temptation). There are also frequent references to pertinent passages in the Old Testament, particularly the prophecies of the coming of John and Jesus. (For examples, see lines 441–50 and 636–43; all passages derived from the Scriptures are identified in the Explanatory Notes.) Nothing of importance from the Gospel accounts has been omitted from the play, and the author often translates or paraphrases them directly. (For examples, see lines 166–72 and 277–86.) A rough calculation reveals that about 250 of the play's 1000 lines derive from the Scriptures in this manner.

At the same time, the author has subjected the Gospel accounts to an enormous process of amplification, with the result that the Scriptures constitute only one of the several important classes of sources for the play. We may see this most clearly if we note that of the nine "scenes" into which the play is divided, only four owe any substantial verbal or narrative debt to the Scriptures. These are John's Preaching ("Scene 2"), the Baptism itself (4), the Interrogation of John by the Jews (6), and the Temptation of Jesus by Satan (8). For the rest of his play the author has turned to other materials, sometimes suggested or hinted at by the Gospels, but often entirely outside the scriptural tradition.

3.3 *Apocryphal Gospels*

3.3.1 The distinction between "apocryphal"—that is, unauthorized or unrecognized—gospels and those now acknowledged as authentic had not yet been made in the Middle Ages. It is consequently not surprising to find the author of *The Baptism and Temptation* supplementing the material furnished by the four Evangelists with other information collected from what we now know were much later writers. The principal "apocryphal" source used by our author was one that was widely influential on all of medieval literature, the *Acts of Pilate*, or, as it was more commonly called, the *Gospel of Nicodemus.*

3.3.2 The first part of the *Acts of Pilate* was written in the fourth century A.D. to refute alleged pagan records of Christ's trial before Pilate. Its purpose is to present what purports to be contemporary evidence of Christ's divinity. The author of the work is, supposedly, the Pharisee Nicodemus, who in the canonical Gospels is reported to have helped in the burial of the body of Jesus (John 3 : 19) and who in our play is represented as having been an early disciple of John the Baptist. The second, and more influential, part of the work furnished the story of the "Harrowing of Hell," widely dramatized in medieval Passion plays.

The *Acts of Pilate* furnished the author of *The Baptism and Temptation* with various details with which to flesh out the Gospel story of John the Baptist's preaching. In particular it provided him with names for the anonymous "disciples" who are mentioned in the Gospels as having been baptized by John (John 1 : 35). In the absence of other biblical evidence, our author has assumed that these disciples were the twelve defenders of Jesus at his trial as recorded by the *Acts.* The relevant passage is as follows:

> Then said certain of them that stood by, devout men of the Jews: We say not that he came of fornication; but we know

> that Joseph was betrothed unto Mary, and he was not born of fornication. . . . Then said they which said that he was not born of fornication, even Lazarus, Asterius, Antonius, Jacob, Amnes, Zeras, Samuel, Isaac, Phinees, Crispus, Agrippa, and Judas: We were not born proselytes, but we are children of Jews and we speak the truth; for verily we were present at the espousals of Joseph and Mary.[1]

Around the names of Lazarus ("Lazay")—not to be confused with the Lazarus raised from the dead by Jesus—Jacob, Zeras, Samuel, Phineas, and Nicodemus, our author has created (with help from the canonical Gospels which record the actual names of John's other early adherents, Andrew and Nathanael) the second and third scenes of his drama, representing the conversion of the Pharisees and "Noblemen" by John the Baptist.

3.4 *The Fathers of the Church*

3.4.1 A good many of the embellishments on scriptural sources, and at least one important incident, in *The Baptism and Temptation* may be traced to patristic commentaries and legends, as handed down through later medieval writings. The principal works through which patristic writings reached medieval dramatists were Peter Comestor's *Historia scholastica* (1198), Jacobus de Voragine's *Legenda aurea* (c. 1255), Vincent of Beauvais's *Speculum majus* (1264), Thomas Aquinas's *Summa theologica* (1274), and Nicholas de Lyre's *Postilles* (1349). Our author may have been familiar with some or all of these. It is likely, however, that he drew the patristic material for his play from his two major literary sources, the pseudo-Bonaventure *Meditationes vitae Christi* and the *Vita Christi* of Ludolphus de Saxonia, where the Fathers are copiously quoted (see below, 3.5). Whatever his immediate sources, the writings of the Fathers furnished him with the basic theological tenets of his play.

In particular, the sermons of Saint John Chrysostom and Saint Jerome provide the ultimate source for the theology of

1. *The Apocryphal New Testament*, ed. M. James, pp. 98–99.

baptism which is rendered so explicit in the first half of the drama. Such ideas as the consubstantiality of God the Father and God the Son (191–93) and baptism as the abolition of circumcision (295–303), such liturgical practices as baptism in the name of the Trinity (29–30, 358–60), and even such imagined incidents as Jesus's baptism of Saint John (337–68) may all be traced to the writings of Chrysostom and Jerome. It was Chrysostom, for example, in his *Homily 12 on Matthew*, who first argued the probability of Jesus having baptized John, although the event is not recorded in the Bible.

A full list of patristic sources of individual passages in our play is included in the Explanatory Notes. Here we may simply cite one longer excerpt from Jerome's *Homily for Epiphany* to suggest the essential theological meaning that the Baptism held for our author:

> His [Jesus's] identity was revealed at the time when He came to the Jordan to be baptized by John the Baptist, and the voice of the Father was heard thundering from heaven: "This is my beloved Son, in whom I am well pleased." The Father had proclaimed Him by His voice from the heavens, and the Holy Spirit, settling upon His head in the form of a dove, ordained to make Him known by that revelation, lest the people mistake anyone else for the Son of God. What is more sublime than His humility, more noble than His belittlement? He is baptized by His servant and He is named Son of God. Along with publicans, prostitutes, and sinners, He came for baptism, and He is holier than the one who baptizes. He is purified by John in the flesh, but he purifies John in the spirit. The waters that had been wont to cleanse others are now purified by the cleansing of our Lord.[2]

3.5 *Meditative Lives of Christ*

3.5.1 By far the most important literary influences on *The Baptism and Temptation* are the two popular, late medieval meditations on the Life of Christ, the Pseudo-Bonaventure *Medita-*

2. Jerome, *The Homilies of Saint Jerome*, trans. M. Ewald, p. 229.

tiones vitae Christi, written by a Franciscan monk in Tuscany around 1275 and attributed during the Middle Ages to Saint Bonaventure, and the *Vita Christi* of Ludolphus de Saxonia, a Carthusian who flourished in the last quarter of the fourteenth century. The technique of both these works is the expansion of the Gospel narrative by means of fictional dialogue and narration, inspired by meditation on the scriptural events. Both works exerted widespread influence on the drama,[3] and it is almost exclusively to them that our author owes his most "original" scenes, in particular those involving the Virgin Mary.

3.5.2 *The "Meditationes."* Part of "Scene 4" and all of "Scene 9" in *The Baptism and Temptation* derive from the Pseudo-Bonaventure *Meditationes*. Lines 235–58 of our text present a touching tableau in which Jesus goes to his mother to say farewell before beginning his public mission. This incident is based on the following passage in the *Meditationes:*

> Imagine the Lord Jesus, having completed His twenty-ninth year . . . saying to His mother, "The time is come that I should glorify and manifest My Father, and show myself to the world, and labour for the salvation of souls, for which the Father sent Me forth. Be of good courage, therefore, good mother, for I shall quickly return to you;" and the Master of lowliness, kneeling down, prayed for a blessing on His departure. And she likewise knelt down, and embracing Him with tears, said most tenderly, "My Blessed Son, go, with a Divine blessing, from your home; be mindful of me, and remember that you soon return to me."[4]

The Ministry of the Angels and the episode of Mary's "supper," which occupy the last scene of our play (845–1014), are

3. For the influence of the *Meditationes* and the *Vita Christi* on French drama, see A. Jeanroy, "Sur quelques sources des mystères de la Passion," and E. Mâle, *L'art religieux de la fin du Moyen Age en France*, pp. 35–51; on English drama, R. Woolf, *The English Mystery Plays*, pp. 159–237.

4. [Pseudo-Bonaventure], *Meditationes vitae Christi*, trans. W. H. Hutchings, chap. 16.

perhaps our author's most striking additions to traditional dramatic treatments of the Temptation in the Wilderness. But once again we find the scene closely modeled on the *Meditationes:*

> When he had completed the victory, Angels came and ministered unto Him. . . . And what, I ask, did the angels bring Him to eat after so long a fast? The Scriptures do not tell us. We may, therefore, picture this victorious repast as our devotion leads us. . . . The Angels say to Him, "O Lord, Thou has fasted much; what wilt Thou that we shall make ready for Thee?" And some have imagined Him replying, "Go to My dearest Mother, and if she has anything prepared, bring it to Me; for of no food do I eat with such pleasure as of that which comes from her hand. . . ." The same legend says they bore away some pottage which she had prepared for herself and Joseph, and some bread, with a table cloth, and other necessaries; and perhaps the Blessed Mother purchased a few small fish, as far as her means allowed, which also we can imagine that they took with them. . . . When He reached His home, doubtless His Mother, seeing Him, arose at once to greet Him with inexpressible delight, and received Him in her arms with the closest embraces; and He next greeted her, and also His foster-father Joseph, and, perhaps, abode with them as of yore a brief while.[5]

To this account our author has added some extra details from chapter 22 in Ludolphus: God's order to two angels to go to Mary, to report Christ's victory, and to bring him her supper, and the bringing of manna from heaven along with the supper.

3.5.3 *The "Vita Christi."* Much of Ludolphus de Saxonia's *Vita Christi* is based on Pseudo-Bonaventure, but a number of details in our play, such as those just mentioned in the account of the angelic ministry, are unique to the later work, suggesting that our author consulted each one separately. To Ludol-

5. Ibid., chap. 17.

phus he owes the idea of the Baptism as the first public manifestation of the Trinity (31–37) and the definition of the purpose of the baptism of Jesus (218–26). From Ludolphus too come such incidents as the presence of the angels at the Baptism (300 SD)—angels are not mentioned in the Gospel accounts—as well as Jesus's descent from the pinnacle of the Temple via a "gate" and a staircase (779–82). In addition, we may find in Ludolphus's verbal descriptions the visual content of some of the silent tableaux which our author has only hinted at in his stage directions, as in the following account of Jesus eating his "supper" (cf. 951 SD):

> Les anges disposent le repas sur le sol et Jésus-Christ bénit solennellement la nourriture. Ah! Considérez-le attentivement ici dans tous les détails de sa conduite; il s'assied à terre dans une attitude grave et modeste, il mange avec sobriété; considérez aussi les anges: ils environment leur Maître pour le servir; ils chantent un hymne des cantiques de Sion, ils se livrent à la jubilation. . . . Toutefois leur joie est mêlée d'une tristesse à laquelle nous devrions prendre part; ils considèrent Jésus avec les sentiments pleins de respect, et en voyant leur Dieu et leur Seigneur, celui qui donne la nourriture à tout être vivant, aussi humilié, ayant besoin de se faire donner la nourriture corporelle et de manger comme un simple mortel, ils sont saisis de compassion.[6]

3.6 *Other plays.* As noted above (2.1.4), *The Baptism and Temptation* contains a number of unique features not to be found in other surviving medieval Passion plays but which presumably derive from its now-lost original, the first day of the *Passion d'Auvergne.* Among existing plays only the *Passion de Semur* bears any resemblance to our play, though the resemblance is slight. Of contact with the Gréban-Michel Passion play tradition there is no evidence whatsoever. That our author was theatrically experienced and well acquainted with medieval dra-

6. Ludolphus, *Vita Iesu Christi*, trans. M. P. Augustin, chap. 22.

matic conventions, however, is apparent not only in his skill as a playwright but in his introduction of certain traditional theatrical scenes and motifs into his play.

3.6.1 *The Gréban and Michel Passions.* The independence of our play from the Gréban-Michel tradition may be seen at a glance. Although Gréban begins the second day of his *Passion* at the same point as our play, and although he covers much of the same material, the sequence of scenes is different, some are omitted (notably the Council of the Jews and the Ministry of the Angels), and there are no verbal resemblances between the two plays. The Michel *Passion* is somewhat closer in structure to our play, but again there are no signs of direct borrowing. Michel begins his first day with John the Baptist's preaching, but God the Father does not appear in the scene and there are no verbal resemblances, beyond some inevitable biblical echoes. The Council of the Jews follows ("Scene 5" of our play), but Herod does not appear, and of the ten Pharisees and Sadducees who do appear in the scene not a single one bears the name of any character in our play. The Interrogation of John and Jesus's farewell to his mother follow a different order than in our play and again reveal no verbal similarities. Mary's part is greatly expanded by our author at this point: Michel writes in a stage direction that "demeure Nostre Dame seule comme en oroison" ("Our Lady remains alone as if in prayer"), while in our play she is given a moving prayer imploring the safety of her son (259–70). The Baptism and the Temptation scenes proper show no resemblance in the two works and in fact contain different emphases. In our play God the Father beholds the Baptism with almost human paternal delight—"Se qu'il fait m'est doulx counme cresme" ("What he has done is as sweet to me as cream" [306])—while in Michel he harangues the audience with scholastic theology:

> Je veul, par ung signe haultain,
> Monstrer en divine puissance
> Signe evident et congnoiscance
> De nostre unie trinité
> Et de nostre trine unité,

> Et aparoir sensiblement
> Ad ce tres sainct baptisement,
> Ung en troys especes sensibles.
> [2084–91][7]

It is my will to show forth, through my divine power and by means of a heavenly sign, a visible symbol and token of our united trinity and of our triune unity, and to appear visibly at this holy baptism, One God in three physical elements.

Similarly, in the Temptation scene Michel's Jesus is a holy stoic—"Ainsi passeray mes sejours/ En jeune et devote oroyson" ("Thus I shall spend my days in fasting and devout prayer" [2194–95])—while the Jesus in our play speaks volubly of his pain and suffering (compare lines 700–25 below). The last part of Michel's sequence parallels the structure of our play more closely than does Gréban, but still without significant similarities. Berith, a Pharisee in our play, appears as a devil in Michel's Council in Hell. In Michel the other angels minister to Jesus while Gabriel tends to Mary, there is no mention of a "supper," and the reunion of Jesus and Mary is dispatched in a mere seventeen lines.

3.6.2 *The "Passion de Semur."* We may conclude, then, that *The Baptism and Temptation of Christ* belongs to a Passion play tradition independent of the Gréban-Michel manuscripts which exerted such influence in the north of France. The evidence connecting our play with the *Passion d'Auvergne* and with a performance at Montferrand, near modern-day Clermont-Ferrand, suggests that this alternate tradition originated in the *midi* and passed through Auvergne and Burgundy until reaching the stage preserved in our manuscript. The Burgundian associations may be traced in the *Passion de Semur*, which, though hardly identical with our play, bears some faint traces of having been influenced by a manuscript in the same tradition. This work, which is preserved in a manuscript copied in

7. J. Michel, *Le mystère de la Passion*, ed. O. Jodogne.

Burgundy in 1488, bears more verbal similarities to our play than do either the Michel or the Gréban plays. While in structure it is totally different from our play, covering the events from the Creation of the World to the Temptation in its first day and the rest of the Passion story in its second, the *Passion de Semur* reveals occasional echoes of our play, chiefly in its character-names. John the Baptist, for example, is arrested by Beric and Nachor (cf. Berith and Natort in our play), characters who do not appear in these roles in any other play (in Michel, Berith is a devil). Similarly, we find the name Nason used for a disciple of John, as in our play, whereas in Michel this name is used for a henchman of Herod. Even more intriguing is the appearance in the *Passion de Semur* of Malifferas, a character-name unknown elsewhere, as a servant of the Archbishop in the episode of the marriage of Joseph and Mary. Of the disciples of John in our play, two (Nathanael and Andrew) are omitted from *Semur*, but the other two, Samuel and Nason, are identically named—again a feature that cannot be paralleled in other plays. While these are slight similarities, they are nonetheless striking and may indicate that the two plays descend from a common original.

3.6.3 There is abundant evidence of more general theatrical influences, other than those involving specific texts. Our author was clearly familiar not only with dramatic treatments of the Passion story but with the conventions and motifs of medieval drama as a whole. The scene of the Council in Hell, for which no single literary or theological source exists, was common to almost all medieval dramatic treatments of the Passion, both in England and in France. The characterization of Annas and Caiaphas as contemporary in age, sharing the authority of the office of High Priest, and participating equally in the condemnation of Christ, is a commonplace in medieval literature and drama, though it is at odds with the Gospel narratives, in which Caiaphas is the sole High Priest at the time of Jesus's arrest, having inherited the office from his father-in-law, Annas. And such incidents as Malifferas's compulsion to stop for a drink on his journey to Herod (545) and his habitual running out of breath while on his embassies (425)—incidents which were possibly accompanied by much improvised business and dialogue—suggest the influence of the farce and other types of secular plays, in which soldiers are commonly drunk and messengers habitually late (see the explanatory note on line 545).

4 Language

4.1 The language of *The Baptism and Temptation of Christ* is characteristic of late Middle French, that is, the late fifteenth or more probably the early sixteenth century. By this time many of the major provincial dialectal variations had disappeared, and the standardization of written French was well advanced. This stage of French is well known, and since the text presents few difficulties, there is no need for a detailed study of the language of the play. This chapter has two purposes: (1) to examine in some depth those elements of the language which can help to date and locate the text more precisely; and (2) to comment on those aspects of the text which appear to be of special linguistic significance.

4.2 *Author and scribe.* Little is to be gained by separating the study of the language of the scribe from that of the author. As will be seen below, they both appear to share the same dialect, since the spellings used by the scribe are consonant with the author's own language as reflected in the rhymes and scansion. This is not to say, however, that our MS preserves the original version of the play; indeed, the versification indicates that the scribe copied his MS from an already existing model, and that, in doing so, he has unconsciously introduced several minor modifications (see below, 5.1.3). That the time which elapsed between the composition of the original and the redaction of the present manuscript was short is proved by the fact that the dialects of the scribe and the poet are virtually indistinguishable.

4.3 *Dating by statistical analysis.* Middle French (from the fourteenth to the sixteenth centuries) was a period of gradual linguistic change, when many so-called etymological or old forms were replaced by analogical or new forms. Previous work[1] has shown that by calculating the frequency of certain key linguistic forms in undated texts and by comparing the results with those obtained from similar but dated texts it is possible to arrive at an approximate date for the text in question. The four linguistic points concerned are: (1) the use of the Old French nominative case (*cas-sujet*) in masculine nouns; e.g., *amis* as opposed to *ami;* (2) first person singular present tense forms; e.g., *je port–je porte; je vien–je viens;* (3) adjectives which were invariable for gender in Old French; e.g., feminine *fort–forte, tel–telle;* (4) mute *e* in hiatus before a tonic vowel; e.g., *seür–sur, deüsse–dusse.* The versification will often show whether the author used the older or the newer alternative. The greater the overall use of new forms, the more recent the text. The figures obtained for *The Baptism and Temptation* are as follows: (1) use of Old French nominatives attested by versification: 0 percent of cases; (2) use of etymological first person singular present tense forms: 5 percent of cases; (3) use of invariable feminine adjectives: 50 percent of cases; (4) retention of hiatus of mute *e* before a tonic vowel: 0 percent of cases. The average of these four percentages, 0, 5, 50, 0, is 14 percent. These results are similar to those obtained from an analysis of Gringore's *Vie de Saint Louis* of 1512 and suggest that the present play is unlikely to have been composed before the sixteenth century. A fuller explanation of the dating system used, and its application to a score of late medieval French plays, appears in the relevant articles.[2]

4.4 *Details of special interest*

4.4.1 *Phonetic/orthographic.*

(a) *o/ou.* Perhaps the most striking linguistic feature of the text is the high frequency of the spelling *ou* in words where

1. G. Runnalls, "The Linguistic Dating of Middle French Texts." See also Runnalls, ed., *Le mystère de la Passion Nostre Seigneur*, pp. 23–27.

2. Ibid.

standard French had *o*, e.g., *repouser* for *reposer* (1004). This suggests phonetically that the open and close *o* had closed to [u]; numerous rhymes support this view, as well as indicating that this pronunciation was common to both scribe and playwright; e.g., *moutz* (=*mots*) : *tous* (282–83) : *nous* (500–01) : *doulx* (700–02). The rhymes also suggest that even the letter *o* was pronounced in the same way: *hocte* (= *hotte*) : *socte* (= *sotte*) : *doubte* (792–94); cf. also *pouvres* : *autres* (165–66). *ou* for *o* is found in all phonetic contexts; e.g., pretonic: *vouler* (27), *ouster* (162), *consouler* (236), *lougee* (606); tonic: *vous* (= *vos*) (172), *voustre* (43), *chouses* (332), etc. The phenomenon of *ouisme*, as it has been called, is discussed in all the major reference works on the language of the early sixteenth century.[3] Though some early examples, in a small number of phonetic contexts, are found at the end of the fifteenth century, *ouisme* only becomes widespread in the sixteenth. Originating in the center of France, in the Loire valley and the province of Berry, the pronunciation was taken up by the court in Paris and became highly fashionable. The *Passion d'Auvergne* itself has a fair amount of *ouisme*.

(b) *er/ar*. Both spelling and rhyme show that *e* and *a* were confused when they occurred before *r*; e.g., *desert* : *part* : *escart* (378–81); *guerre* : *dessarre* : *acquerre* : *terre* (709–14); *pardre* (593) : *perdre* : *arde* (618–19), etc. It is difficult to say whether the vowel actually used was *e* or *a*, though it was probably *a*. The confusion of these two vowels before *r* began as early as Old French but remained in Paris as late as the sixteenth century.[4]

(c) *oi/oy/oe/oue/ouy*. The diphthong pronounced [oi] in Old French and [wɛ] in Middle French is spelled in five different ways by the scribe. *oi* and *oy* are the most frequent:

3. M. Pope, *From Latin to Modern French*, para. 581; F. Brunot, *Histoire de la langue française*, 2 : 254; C. Beaulieux, *Histoire de l'orthographe française*, p. 167 ff.; C. Thurot, *De la prononciation française depuis le commencement du XVIe siècle*, 1 : 240–42; G. Lote, *Histoire du vers français*, 3 : 303–04.

4. See Pope, *From Latin*, para. 496; Thurot, *La prononciation française*, 1 : 3; Lote, *Vers français*, 3 : 290–91; Brunot, *La langue française*, 2 : 249.

devoir (482) : *veoir* (483), etc. *ouy*, as found in *voulouyr* (480) and *chouysir* (900), is fundamentally the same, but also shows the influence of *ouisme* (see [a] above); *oe*, as in *voere* (879), and *oue*, as in *glouere* (88), *douevent* (214), *procuratoueres* (672), *Babillouene* (813), etc., are perhaps more accurate reflections of the scribe's pronunciation. According to Beaulieux[5] this orthography is found as early as the late fifteenth century, but is especially frequent in the sixteenth. The pronunciation [wɛ] is attested not only by the spellings *oe* and *oue* but also by rhymes in [ɛ] : e.g., *voise : plaise* (701–03), etc.

(d) *eu/u*. Rhymes show that *eu* is often confused with *u;* e.g., *heure : procure : demeure* (660–68); *joyeuse : eusse* (923–24); *huche : apreuche* (20–21), etc. According to Lote[6] the confusion of these two sounds, of provincial origin, is especially common in the sixteenth century.

(e) *age/aige*. Before the voiced denti-palatal fricative, *a* raised to *e*, often spelled *ai;* hence rhymes like *lignage : donrré je* (375–76). This is a common phenomenon from the fifteenth century onwards.[7]

(f) *eau*. The Old French triphthong is always spelled *eau*, never *iau* as is often found in Parisian and Northeastern texts of the fourteenth and fifteenth centuries.

(g) *gn*. The palatal *n* is normally spelled *gn*, but two alternative orthographies are used by the scribe: *gnh* in *mignhons* (898) and *nnh* in *Bourgonnhe* (811). In the middle of the sixteenth century, when several scholars were attempting to reform French spelling, J. Pelletier du Mans recommended that *nh* should be used to represent the palatal *n*.[8] The spellings *mignhons* and *Bourgognhe* are found in the *Passion d'Auvergne*.

(h) *h*. The scribe often uses *h* as a device to distinguish two separate vowels from a diphthong; e.g., *crehateur* (259), *prohesse* (317), *louhange* (769), *crehature* (821), etc.

5. See *L'orthographe française*, pp. 173 and 296 ff.
6. See *Vers français*, 3 : 299–301.
7. See Pope, *From Latin*, para. 494.
8. See Thurot, *La prononciation française*, 2 : 301–07, 311, 348.

(i) Other spellings of interest are *fuons* (= *fuions*) (825); *tiel*, *tieulx* (329–30); *mervilleus* (430). These are mostly of Northeastern origin.[9]

(j) The scribe frequently, though not always, uses an unusual digraph to represent the palatal *l*. Similar digraphs are found in some Auvergne manuscripts of the late fifteenth and early sixteenth centuries; but see chapter 7.2.b.

4.4.2 *Morphological.*

(a) *que* for *qui*. For the subject case relative pronoun, *qui* is used only for masculine singular and plural (82, 100, 104, 109, etc.); *que* is also used for the masculine singular and plural (307, 752, 960, 964). *Que* is the normal form for feminine singular and plural (31, 440, 597) and for the neuter (428). Brunot[10] comments that this usage starts as early as the fourteenth century and continues until the sixteenth.

(b) *se/si* (= if). The usual form found in this text is not *se* but *si*. Since it occurs not only before a consonant (140, 468, 500, etc.) but also before a vowel without elision (67, 437), it is clear that *si* is the form preferred both by the scribe and the playwright. If the playwright had used *se*, it would have elided before a vowel, and any modernization of the scribe would show up in the scansion. The older form, *se*, occurs twice only, before consonants (738, 995). According to Rydberg,[11] *si* begins to replace *se* at the very end of the fifteenth century and becomes widespread in the early sixteenth.

(c) *t euphonique*. One example is found of the so-called *t euphonique*, inserted to avoid a hiatus between an inverted verb and subject pronoun: *et ne parlet on que de luy* (463); elsewhere such hiatuses are left intact: *m'a on dit* (462). Thurot[12] states that in the sixteenth century "cette in-

9. See Pope, *From Latin*, paras. 492, 494.
10. See *La langue française*, 2 : 317.
11. G. Rydberg, *Geschichte des französischen e*, pp. 979–91.
12. See *La prononciation française*, 2 : 240–43.

tercalation du *t* n'était pas encore d'un usage exclusif et universel."

(d) *Second person plural endings of verbs.* The scribe regularly uses the ending *-és*, and not *-ez* (1, 8, etc.). But *faictez* occurs twice (138, 679).

(e) *toy/ty.* One example of *ty* is found attested by the rhyme (371); the normal form is *toy. Ty* is of Northeastern origin.

4.5 *Conclusion*

4.5.1 *Place of origin of text.* Because of the increasing standardization of French, especially of the written language, it is difficult to locate the geographical area from which this text came. Indeed, as Lote[13] shows in his study of Middle French pronunciation and morphology as illustrated in contemporary versification, the early sixteenth century permitted much freedom of usage. Dialect forms traveled far from their region of origin, and poets everywhere benefited from them, as well as from other uncertainties or fashions in pronunciation, as they facilitated the task of versifying. It is therefore risky to read too much linguistic significance into one or two isolated forms. *The Baptism and Temptation* could well be from the Auvergne itself, though some forms suggest a more Northern provenance. The most striking regular feature of this text, the *ouisme*, started in the center of France and the Loire, but became fashionable in Paris.

4.5.2 *Date of composition.* The statistical study and the examination of the individual features in the previous sections coincide in pointing to a date toward the early part of the first half of the sixteenth century.[14] This dating is supported by the study of the watermarks and other palaeographic evidence (see 1.2, above).

13. See *Vers français,* 3 : 321–33.

14. If indeed the play was composed in Paris (see 4.5.1), the *terminus ante quem* would be 1548, when the performance of mystery plays was prohibited by the Paris Parlement.

5 Versification

5.1 *Scansion*

5.1.1 In discussing the scansion of late medieval French verse, it is important to remember that traditional practice, together with certain aspects of the pronunciation of Middle French, gave poets considerable freedom, which greatly facilitated the task of composing lines that scanned in an acceptable manner. Certain sounds, for example the mute *e*, could, in certain positions, either count as a syllable or not. The following possibilities should be noted:

(a) *Use or non-use of diaeresis:* Use: *signiffïer* (29), *benedictïon* (60), *devocïons* (76), *virtüeuse* (204), etc. Non-use: *virtueuse* (197), *generacions* (146), *circuncision* (298), *gracieulx* (360), etc.

(b) *Words with double forms: encore* (799)–*encores* (19); *grant* (612)–*grande* (573), etc.

(c) *Mute* e *in hiatus after a tonic or pretonic vowel:* Syllabic value: *vraiement* (551), *singnees* (674), *vouldroie* (893), etc.; Non-syllabic value: *donnees* (677), *vivoient*, *aroient* (117), etc.

(d) *Mute* e *between two consonants:* Syllabic value: *prescheras* (13), *baptiseras* (22), etc. (the more frequent alternative); Non-syllabic value: *lavement* (212), *baptisera* (227), etc.

(e) *Final mute* e *before a vowel:* Elision: *baptesme* (14), *qu'en* (31), etc. (the normal occurrence); Non-elision: *que il baptise en* (554), *autre assalie* (799), etc.

In view of this great flexibility, attested in all late medieval plays, it will be obvious that many lines which are incorrect according to the rules of modern French versification are in fact perfectly acceptable. However, it also becomes difficult to state with confidence whether some lines are metrically acceptable or not. Late medieval scansion was hardly an exact science.

5.1.2 The most frequently used line is the octosyllable, which was the standard line in all medieval theatre. Approximately 800 of the 1014 lines of *The Baptism and Temptation* are octosyllabic. But the poet displays his technical accomplishment in employing many other meters as well: one-syllable lines (510–11), two-syllable (506–08), three-syllable (179, 181, 183, etc.), four-syllable (40–59), five-syllable (837–40), six-syllable (311–26), ten-syllable (818–27).

5.1.3 Even allowing for the flexibility described in 5.1.1, there does appear to be a number of badly scanned lines. These may be attributable to the poet, but it is noticeable that many could be put right with a minor modification. This suggests that they are the results of slips of concentration on the part of the scribe. For example, the freedom to insert or to omit the subject personal pronoun, a characteristic of Middle French, can account for some incorrect lines: adding the pronoun would correct 180, 535, 544, 717, etc.; removing the pronoun would correct 189, 403, 533, 640, etc. Using the alternative form of words with two forms would account for other lines—for example, *quel* for *quelle* (989).

However, certain short passages, which are metrically defective, cannot be corrected by this type of superficial modification: for example, 1–8, 150–56, 815–24.

Overall, given the liberty of metrical practice permitted at the time when the play was composed, the scansion is generally sound, and most of the minor faults can be attributed to scribal interference.

5.2 *Rhyme schemes*

5.2.1 *The octosyllabic couplet* was the basic rhyme scheme used in all medieval French plays from the thirteenth to the sixteenth centuries, and *The Baptism and Temptation* is no exception in this respect. But it is well known that in the fifteenth and sixteenth centuries in particular, dramatists, like their lyric poet contemporaries, became actively interested in the challenge of technical virtuosity in versification, and especially in the use of varied rhyme schemes.

The octosyllabic couplet is the scheme used for less than half (approximately 460 lines) of the surviving 1014 lines of our play. One of the advantages for the dramatist of the octosyllabic couplet, apart from its simplicity, is its suitability for mnemonic rhyming. This was the traditional system of cuing in speakers; the first line of each speech rhymed with the last line of the preceding speech.[1] As long as the author of our play writes in octosyllabic couplets, he links the speeches by mnemonic rhymes (e.g. 8–27, etc.). However, this system of cuing by rhyme becomes less effective when he turns to more complex rhyme schemes stretching over many lines. Over a dozen different schemes are used in our relatively brief fragment.

5.2.2 *Tercets:*[2]

(1) $aa^{8}b^{3}$,$cc^{8}b^{3}$, . . . (615–26)

(2) $aa^{4}b^{8}$, $bb^{3}c^{8}$, $cc^{3}d^{8}$, $dd^{3}e^{8}$, . . . (787–98)

5.2.3 *Quatrains:*

(1) $abab^{8}$, $bcbc^{8}$, . . . (227–30, 301–08, 628–59, 700–23, 747–86, 801–24, 845–60, 869–72, 886–93, 989–96)

(2) $a^{5}b^{6}a^{5}b^{6}$, $bcbc^{6}$, $cdcd^{5}$, $d^{5}ede^{6}$ (829–44)

(3) $abab^{6}$, $bcbc^{6}$, . . . (960–71)

5.2.4 *Cinquains:*

(1) $aabab^{4}$, $ccdcd^{4}$, . . . (40–59)

(2) $ababc^{8}$, $cdcdc^{8}$, $cecec^{8}$, . . . (101–30)

(3) $a^{4}b^{6}a^{4}b^{6}c^{4}$, $b^{4}d^{6}b^{4}d^{6}c^{4}$, $c^{4}e^{6}c^{4}e^{6}f^{4}$. (930–44)

1. This practice is demonstrated by the fact that some medieval plays have survived not in complete form, but in *rooles;* these are the speeches of one character, prepared exclusively for the actor who was to take that particular rôle. Each of the speeches of the character in question is preceded by the crucial mnemonic rhyme, the last line of the previous speaker's speech. See the description of the *Mystère de Sainte Barbe* in J. Chocheyras, *Le théâtre religieux en Savoie*, pp. 91 ff.

2. In the following sections the following conventions are adopted: the letters refer to the rhymes; capital letters indicate the repetition not only of a rhyme but of the whole line. The superscript numbers represent the number of syllables in each line.

(4) . . . $egeg^6f^4$, $fhfh^6i^3$, $hjhj^6i^3$. (945–59)
(5) $aaaaa^6$, $bbbba^6$, $ccdda^6$. (974–88)

5.2.5 *Huitains:*
(1) *triolets:* A B A A A b A B^8. (71–78, 361–68, 662–69; 682–89; 861–68)
(2) $a^8a^3b^8b^3c^8c^3d^8d^3$. (176–83)
(3) $abababab^6$, $cdcdcdcd^6$. (311–26)

5.2.6 *Dixains:*
(1) $abab^4c^8dede^4c^8$, . . . (327–56, 369–98)

5.2.7 *Douzains:*
(1) $ab^8b^3a^8a^3b^8b^8b^3c^8b^8c^3c^8$, . . . (191–226, 259–70, 572–95)

5.2.8 Some single lines are totally isolated and rhyme with no other line; for example, 1, 4, 144, 148, 172, 358, 537, 885. Moreover, there are also several passages of what might be called free or mixed rhyme scheme, where no regular pattern is adhered to: 131–60, 167–73, etc.

5.2.9 *The purpose of the different rhyme schemes.* The complex systems listed above are not simply a decorative testimony to the poet's technical virtuosity; they are also functional. Taking the octosyllabic couplet as the neutral or unmarked verse form, the more complex rhyme patterns have the value of being distinctive and are often used to achieve structural or expressive effects. The introduction of a new scheme frequently marks a change in scene or a passage of heightened importance or emotion. For example, the *triolets* (see 5.2.5.[1], above), through their ritual-like repetitions, point to the end of a section of the action. The major sermons and prayers are always in one of the more complex stanzaic structures, as are most of the angels' scenes and the dialogues between Jesus and the Virgin Mary. The devils' incantations, too, are similarly marked.

5.3 *Rhyme quality.* The poet appears to have paid less attention to the quality of the rhymes than to their structural combinations; perhaps this is the result of the technical demands of the complex rhyme patterns. Most rhymes are simple and minimal (*rimes pauvres ou suffisantes*), and even the richer rhymes are banal and unoriginal, being based, for example, on morphologically related words or derivatives; for example, 30–31, 42–44; 208–10, etc. Indeed, many rhymes are only approximate at best: 20–21, 28–29, 131–32, 165–66, 168–70, 232–33, 434–35; 645–47, 664–65, etc. There are also several lines which rhyme with no other; see 5.2.8.

One curious rhyme tends to support the view expressed in 5.1.3 that some of the defects in the versification may be the result of scribal interference. At lines 454–55, *vie* is supposed to rhyme with *Jacaret*, obviously not an acceptable rhyme. But elsewhere in the text, the name of John the Baptist's father is given not as *Jacaret*, but as *Zacarie* (e.g., 6); *Zacarie*, of course, makes an adequate rhyme with *vie*. It would appear that the scribe, in copying from his source, unconsciously replaced the correct name by its more familiar French version.

5.4 In sum, the versification is of uneven quality. Although much effort and ingenuity have been devoted to the devising and intelligent use of the many complex rhyme schemes, the actual rhymes used are often hardly more than adequate. Moreover, the scansion is occasionally irregular, though some of these latter defects may well be the fault of the scribe.

6 Note on the Text and Translation

6.1 In editing *The Baptism and Temptation of Christ* we have scrupulously respected the text of the MS wherever it bears an acceptable interpretation (faulty rhymes included). Corrections have been made only where there is an obvious error; these corrections, numbering only twelve, are indicated by an asterisk in the text. The rejected MS readings are given in parentheses in the margin beside the line in question. With regard to the use of diacritical signs, capitals, and punctuation, we have generally followed the recommendations of the 1925 Congrès des Romanistes (see *Romania* 1926). The acute accent is used to indicate tonic *e* in final position or before *s* in polysyllabic words; a diaeresis serves to show a hiatus where the scansion justifies it.

6.2 *Features of the scribe's handwriting affecting the transcription* (we are referring here exclusively to Scribe A; see 1.2.3 above):

(a) The scribe does not employ frequent abbreviations—much less than in earlier MSS—and when he does use them, they are the simplest ones: a bar to indicate a nasal consonant, a *p* with a line below for *par/per*, *Jhs* with a horizontal line above for *Jhesus*, etc. These have been transcribed in the usual way.

(b) The most unusual feature is the digraph indicating the palatal *l*. Although on three occasions (63, 69, 102) the scribe merely uses a double *l* (e.g., *despoullés*), on the other thirty-five occasions that the palatal *l* occurs, he uses a digraph made up of a simple *l* followed by another *l* with a tail curving to the left. This second element, which could also be described as a capital *j*, is also used on one occasion (917) as a normal *l* in *seul*. The upper parts of the two letters in question are not loops but straight lines: . Prou[1] transcribes a similar digraph in a Puy-de-Dôme register of 1521 by *lh*, but this is a manuscript where the standard *h* is identical with the second element of the digraph—not the case in the *Harvard Passion*. We have finally decided to transcribe it by a plain double *l*, and to list here all its occurrences: 66, 67, 185, 189, 190 SD, 275, 277, 342, 346 SD, 389, 407, 430, 432, 456, 460, 496, 542, 648, 650, 669, 691, 692, 774, 780, 785, 841, 846, 882, 891, 892, 896, 923, 946, 1006, 1007.

(c) *i/j*. The voiced denti-palatal fricative (Modern French *j*) is written by the scribe either as *j* (in word-initial position) or as *g* (initially before *e* or *i*, or medially); for example, *je* (84), *gens* (16), *jeune* (707), *mangast* (889). The only exception is *tousiours* (159, 247, 1004), which we transcribe as *tousjours*. The vowel *i* in initial position is written either as *i* or as *j*; we adopt modern spelling practice in this edition.

(d) *c/s*. The scribe uses indifferently either *c* or *s* before *e* to represent the voiceless sibilant; for example, *se que* (=*ce que*, 10), *cellon* (=*selon*, 176), *ses* (=*ces*, 731), *ces* (=*ses*, 760). We have retained the scribe's spelling.

(e) Other aspects of the scribe's usage, which are of linguistic interest, are discussed in chapter 4.

6.3 The text of this edition is presented in such a way as to resemble as closely as possible the appearance of the pages of the MS. Names of speakers and stage directions are italicized and stage directions are placed to the left or to the right of the column of text, as in the MS. In addition, we have italicized words in Latin, and placed in brackets the stage directions of

1. M. Prou, *Recueil de fac-similés* (Paris, 1904), 3 : 42.

Scribe B (see 1.2.3 above). No other stage directions have been added. Folio numbers have been included in the printed text.

6.4 The text is accompanied by a translation into modern English which has no literary pretensions in itself, but which seeks to provide both an accurate and a readable rendering of the original. The inclusion of such a translation makes a glossary unnecessary, as does the fact that very few lexical items in the 1014 lines of the play are not also attested in the standard Middle French dictionaries: Godefroy, Tobler-Lommatsch, and, especially, Huguet. The few problematic passages and lexical items are discussed in the explantory notes on the text. The translation is complete, except for such terms as *silete* and *pausa*, the meaning of which is in dispute and which have accordingly been left untranslated (see above, 2.3.4).

The Baptism and Temptation of Christ

Characters

Characters are listed here in the order in which they appear in the play. Spellings represent the most frequent usage in the manuscript. Names in brackets are English equivalents used in the translation. Names for which no familiar equivalents exist have been retained in the original French forms. Brief descriptions of each character's function in the play are provided and follow the text as closely as possible. Numbers in parentheses indicate the line at which each character speaks for the first time. For further information on the characters, see the Explanatory Notes.

RAPHAEL, an Archangel (1)
DIEU LE PERE [GOD THE FATHER] (9)
SAINT JEHAN [SAINT JOHN THE BAPTIST] (11)
SAMUEL, a Disciple of John (61)
SAINT ANDRIEU [SAINT ANDREW], a Disciple of John (65)
NATANAEL [NATHANAEL], a Disciple of John (71)
NASON, a Disciple of John (74)
JOSEPH DE ARIMATHIE [JOSEPH OF ARIMATHAEA], a Nobleman (101)
JACOB, a Nobleman (106)
ZERAS, a Nobleman (111)
NYCODEMUS [NICODEMUS], a Pharisee (116)
FINES [PHINEAS], a Pharisee (121)
LAZAY, a Pharisee (126)
JHESUS [JESUS] (191)
MARIE [MARY], Mother of Jesus (241)
GABRIEL, an Archangel (309)
HERODES [HEROD], King of Judaea (403)
MALIFFERAS, Herod's Messenger (405)
CAIAPHAS, a High Priest (409)

ANNAS, a High Priest (415)
NATORT, a Pharisee (417)
BERITH, a Pharisee (419)
LUCIFER, Prince of Hell (565)
SATHAN [SATAN], a Devil (569)
BELZEBUT [BEELZEBUB], a Devil (616)
ASTAROT [ASHTORETH], a Devil (619)
ASMO, a Devil (622)
URIEL, an Archangel (879)

CROWD
ANGELS

(28 speaking parts)

S'enscuivent les nongs des personnas et la quantité du premier dimanche, escript premierement: 1a

—Deus pater cum barba grisca et cappa et habeat tres coronas / supra caput; et habeat in manu (sceptrum)./

—Item: sanctus Johannis cum magna barba / et cum raupa facta ex pillis chamelli.

RAPHAEL 2a

1 Or conmancés, mes conpaignons;
Feisons a noustre Dieu joyeux rondel.

Cantus comunis.

Concinamus nato Emanuel.

4 Es cieulx menons grant joye.
Dieu eternel en terre a tramis
Jehan Zacarie, precurseur de son filz,
Pleisant es anges, nuysant es ennemys,
8 Disant: venés en gloere!

DIEU LE PERE

Escoute, Jehan, mectz en memoyre
Se que feras a mon pleisir.

Lors seint Jehan se met a genoulx devant Dieu le pere et dit a meins joinctes:

S. JEHAN

O vray Dieu, donne moy loysir
12 D'aconplir ton conmandement.

DIEU LE PERE

Tu prescheras d'or en avant
Baptesme et seincte penictance,
Paix, boncté, doulceur et clemance,
16 Es gens de franche volanté.

Here follow the names of the characters and the contents of the first Sunday, and first of all:

—God the Father with a gray beard and a hooded cloak, and let him have three crowns on his head; and let him hold a sceptre in his hand.

—Item: Saint John with a long beard and with a robe made of camel's hair.

RAPHAEL

1 Now begin, my friends;
Let us sing a joyful rondeau to our Lord.

The chorus sings.

Concinamus nato Emanuel.
4 Let us rejoice in heaven.
Eternal God has sent to earth
John, the son of Zachariah, to prepare the way for his son,
Bringing joy to his angels and harm to his enemies,
8 Saying: come to heavenly glory!

GOD THE FATHER

Listen, John, place in your memory
What you shall do to please me.

Then Saint John kneels before God the Father and says with folded hands:

SAINT JOHN

O, true God, give me permission
12 To accomplish your command.

GOD THE FATHER

From this day forward you shall preach
Baptism and holy penance,
Peace, goodness, meekness and mercy,
16 Among men of good will.

S. JEHAN
Souverein Dieu, plein de bonté,
Je feray ton conmandement.

DIEU LE PERE
Encores feras plus avant,
20 Pour ce que veux que soyes huche
De mon filz qu'ad mourir s'apreuche.
Tu en brief le baptiseras.

S. JEHAN
Hellas, souverein Dieu, hellas!
24 Dy moy conment pourré cognoistre
Ton filz, mon seigneur et mon meistre
(Pour)* le servir et honnourer. (MS déchiré)

DIEU LE PERE 2b
Des cieulx verras sur luy vouler,
28 En le baptisant, la colunbe,
Pour signiffïer la proffunde
Et habundant fructueusité
Qu'en luy est, et la trinité
32 De personnes en unne essance.
Lors tu congnoistras en substance
Moy en ma voix paternelle,
Mon filz en presence charnelle
36 Et en espece colunbine,
Le seint esperit, m'amour fine.
Lieve toy, lesse se desert;
Va t'en prescher en toute part
40 Ce que t'ay dit.

S. JEHAN (*Lors surgit Johannis.*)
Sans contredit
Devoctement
A voustre dit
44 Contentement
Donrré, mon Dieu.

SAINT JOHN
Lord God, full of goodness,
I will carry out your command.

GOD THE FATHER
You shall do still more,
20 Because I wish you to be the herald
Of my son, who will shortly meet his death.
Quickly shall you baptize him.

SAINT JOHN
Alas! Lord God, alas!
24 Tell me how I may recognize
Your son, my Lord and master,
That I may serve and honor him.

GOD THE FATHER
From the heavens above you will see descending upon him,
28 When you baptize him, the dove,
To signify the deep
And abundant fruitfulness
That is in him, and the trinity
32 Of three persons in one essence.
Then shall you perceive in substance
Me and my paternal voice,
My son in fleshly form,
36 And in the form of a dove,
The holy spirit, my pure love.
Rise up; leave this desert;
Go and preach, everywhere,
40 What I have told you.

SAINT JOHN *(Then John rises.)*
Without contradiction,
Piously,
Shall I give
44 Satisfaction
To your command, my God.

DIEU LE PERE
Laisse ce lieu;
Va conmencer!
48 Presche en hebrieu
Pour baptiser
Pres du Jordain.

S. JEHAN
Mon Dieu, demein
52 Feray devoir.

DIEU LE PERE
Sur toy ma mein
Aras pour voir
Pour toy garder.

S. JEHAN *(Lors se mect a genolz.)*
56 Dont sans tarder
Copieusement
Pour moy aider
Benignement
60 Donnés moy benedictïon!

SAMUEL 3a
Puis qu'ausi vous nous advisés,
Pour Dieu, sire, baptisés nous.

S. JEHAN
Je le veux bien; despoullés vous!
64 Et baptesme conmencerons.

S. ANDRIEU
De bon ceur, sire, le ferons,
Puis qu'ausi le nous conseillés.

(Pausa cum silete.)
Tunc expolient se illi iiij[or]*.*
(C'est assavoir Andrieu,
Natanael, Nazon et saint
Samuel.)

GOD THE FATHER
Leave this place;
Go and begin your work!
48 Preach in Hebrew
And baptize
By the Jordan.

SAINT JOHN
My God, tomorrow
52 Shall I begin my service.

GOD THE FATHER
In truth, you shall have
My hand upon you,
To guard you from harm.

SAINT JOHN *(Then he kneels.)*
56 So without delay
Give me your blessing,
Heartily,
Graciously,
60 To aid me.

SAMUEL
For God's sake, sir, baptize us,
Since you instruct us to do so.

SAINT JOHN
I will; disrobe yourselves.
64 And we shall begin the baptism.

SAINT ANDREW
Heartily, sir, shall we do it,
Since you instruct us to do so.

(Pausa cum silete.) Then let these four disrobe themselves. (That is, Andrew, Nathaniel, Nason, and Saint Samuel.)

S. JEHAN
Si en pechés estes soullés,
68 Il faut qu'a Dieu demandés graces,
Puis que vous estes despollés,
Quar seul Dieu les pechés efface.

NATANAEL
Misericorde en ceste place,
72 Vray Dieu, de bon ceur te prïons.

S. JEHAN
Or levés es cieulx voustre face.

NASON
Misericorde en ceste place.

S. JEHAN
Or levés es cieulx voustre face
76 Et moustrés vous devocïons.

S. ANDRIEU, NATANAEL, NASON, ET SAMUEL *simul*
Misericorde en ceste place
Vray Dieu, de bon ceur te crïons.

Johannis ponit aquam supra illos quatuor dicipulos.

S. JEHAN
Dieu vous doint benedictïons,
80 Et affin qu'il vous soit propice,
Au nom de celluy vous baptise
Qui doit venir pour tous sauver.

Tunc induunt vestimenta que despoliaverant illi dicipuli. (*Pausa cum cilete.*)

S. JEHAN
Je vous ay d'eau volu laver
84 Car autre puissance n'ay mye.
Mais le Dieu d'Israel je prie
Qu'i(l) vous doint telle repantance
Et ainsi vivre en penictence
88 Que venir puissiés en sa glouere.

SAINT JOHN
If you are stained with sin,
68 You must ask pardon of God
While you are in your nakedness,
For only God can wipe away sin.

NATHANIEL
Show mercy to us here,
72 True God, we pray heartily to you.

SAINT JOHN
Now raise your eyes to heaven.

NASON
Show mercy to us here.

SAINT JOHN
Now raise your eyes to heaven
76 And show your piety.

SAINT ANDREW, NATHANIEL, NASON AND SAMUEL, *together*
Show mercy to us here,
True God, we cry heartily to you.

John pours water over the four disciples.

SAINT JOHN
May God give you his blessing,
80 And so that he may look kindly upon you,
I baptize you in the name of Him
Who shall come to save all men.

Then the disciples put on the garments they have removed. (Pausa cum cilete.)

SAINT JOHN
I have sought to wash you with water
84 Because no other power belongs to me.
But I pray that the God of Israel
May give you such repentance
And lead you to a life of penitence
88 That you may come into his heavenly glory.

S. ANDRIEU 3b
Tout temps de vous arons memoire
Et vous prenons par noustre meistre.

NATANAEL
Voustre disciple je veux estre.

NASON
92 Aussi fais je.

SAMUEL
Et moy si fais.

S. JEHAN
Mes enfans, tenés vous en paix,
Puis qu'avec moy voulés vivre,
Affin que je puisse parsuivre
96 L'office que Dieu m'a commis.

Tunc vadant ad Bethaniam circa Jordanem. *Pausa modica.*

Alons plus avant, mes amis,
En Israel et en Judee,
Prescher la bonne renonmee
100 Du redempteur qui doit venir.

Cilete.

JOSEPH DE ARIMATIE *parle a ses conpaignons.*
Mes seigneurs, pour entretenir
La coustume de gentillece,
Il seroit bon de aller ouÿr
104 Le prophete qui ja grant piece
A presché du grant Messïas.

Tunc vadant ad Johannem et eundo loquantur sequentia:

SAINT ANDREW
We will ever remember you,
And follow you as our master.

NATHANIEL
I wish to be your disciple.

NASON
92 And so do I.

SAMUEL
And I too.

SAINT JOHN
My children, peace be with you,
Since you wish to live with me
And help me pursue
96 The service which God has entrusted to me.
Then let them go around Jordan to Bethany. *Pausa modica.*
Let us go further, my friends,
To Israel and Judea,
To preach the great fame
100 Of the Savior who shall come.

Cilete.
JOSEPH OF ARIMATHAEA *speaks to his companions.*
My lords, to maintain
The custom of our nobility,
It would be good to go to hear
104 The prophet who already now, for a long time,
Has preached of the great Messiah.
Then let them go to John and let them speak the following as they go:

JACOB LE PREMIER NOBLE
J'ay ouy dire que Hellïas
N'estoit pas si saint en sa vie,
108 Aussi n'estoit Ysaÿas,
Counme se prophete qui crie
Et presche du grant Messïas.

ZERAS LE SEGOND NOBLE
Il n'a livre ne papïas
112 Ne parchemin pour estutier.
Il fait counme Geremïas:
Tout son fait n'est que vice crier
En preschant du grant Messïas.

NYCODEMUS 4a
116 Hollofernes et Gollïas,
S'ilz vivoient, aroient de luy crainte,
Car il crie de Herodïas
Sans flacterie et sans feincte
120 En preschant du grant Messïas.

FINES LE PREMIER PHARISIEN
Il presche: "*Parate vias*"
Et "Faictes trestous penictence."
Il est plus seint que Thobïas,
124 Tant fait peneuse abstinance,
En preschant du grant Messïas.

LAZAY SEGOND PHARISIEN
Nous devons randre *gracïas*
A Dieu, qui le nous a tramis.
128 Alons tost; advansons nos pas.
Nous sounmes pres.

Tunc sanctus Johannis
clamet: a pecheurs, bis.

JOSEPT
Ouez ses critz!

JACOB, THE FIRST NOBLEMAN
I have heard it said that Elijah
Was not so holy in his life,
108 Nor was Isaiah as pure
As this prophet who cries out
And preaches of the great Messiah.

ZERAS, THE SECOND NOBLEMAN
He has neither book nor paper
112 Nor parchment to study.
He acts like Jeremiah:
All his business is to cry out against vice
While preaching of the great Messiah.

NICODEMUS
116 Holofernes and Goliath,
If they were alive, would fear him,
For he denounces Herodias
Without flattery and without deceit,
120 While preaching of the great Messiah.

PHINEAS, THE FIRST PHARISEE
He preaches: "*Parate vias*"
And "All must do penance."
He is more holy than Tobias,
124 Such rigorous abstinence does he practice,
While preaching of the great Messiah.

LAZAY, THE SECOND PHARISEE
We must give thanks
To God, who sent him to us.
128 Let us all go; hurry our steps.
We are all ready.

Then let Saint John
cry out "Ah, Sinners" twice.

JOSEPH
Hear his cries!

Tunc ascultent sanctum Johannem predicantem sequencia:

S. JEHAN

Ego sum vox clamantis!
Counme dit de moy Ysaÿe
132 En son quarantiesme chapitre,
Voulant parler de Dieu le filz.
Le pere le nous a tramys
En terre de son bon vouloir
136 Et veult que soions advertis
Devoctement le recevoir.
Hellas, pecheurs, faitez devoir!
Laissés voustre mauvaise vie
140 Et pechés, dont l'ame est honnye.
Müés voustre mauvais vouloir.
Le baptesme vous faut avoir,
Et faut que soiés penictens,
144 Si la grace voulés trouver
De Dieu qui viendra en brief tempts.
O generacions de serpens, 4b
Ypocrites pharisïens,
148 Pecheurs mauvaix et malereux,
Qui ne doubtés les jugemens
De Dieu, vous estes cuidans
Que pas ne ressussiterés
152 Anprés la mort. Folz errans,
Si ferés. Si, si ferés!
Et puis tresfort pugnis serés
En corps et ame en enfer.
156 La congniee pour vous frapper
Est pres de vous. Vous perirés,
Serpens; ne vous adviserés?
Serés vous tousjours en malice?
160 Advanssés vous. Tantost mourrés!
Faites penitence propice!

Then let them listen to Saint John, preaching as follows:

SAINT JOHN
Ego sum vox clamantis!
As Isaiah wrote of me
132 In his fortieth chapter,
Wishing to speak of God the Son.
The Father has sent Him to us
On earth through His good will
136 And wishes that we be warned
Devoutly to receive him.
Alas, sinners, do your duty!
Leave your evil lives
140 And your sins, by which the soul is brought to shame
Change your evil wills.
You must be baptized,
And become penitent
144 If you wish to find the grace
Of God, who will come to you shortly.
O generation of vipers,
Unbelieving Pharisees,
148 Wicked and evil sinners,
Who do not fear the judgment
Of God, you think
That you will not be resurrected
152 After death. Foolish lost ones,
Indeed you will be; yes you will.
And then greatly shall you be punished
In body and soul in hell.
156 The blow that is to strike you
Is at hand. You shall perish,
Serpents; will you not take warning?
Will you persist in your evil ways?
160 Come here! Soon you shall die!
Do proper penance!

FINES ET LAZAY *simul* a seint Jehan* (MS simil)
Que ferons pour oster noustre vice?
Dy, noustre meistre!

S. JEHAN
Que ferés?
164 De deux roubes l'une donrrés,
Et de vous autres biens, es pouvres!

ZERAS, JACOB *ad sanctum Johannem*
Hellas, et que ferons nous autres,
Pecheurs publitz?

S. JEHAN
Riens plus, amys,
168 Fors penictence dolereuse.

JOSEPT *ad S. Jehan*
Et nous, gentis gens anoblis?

S. JEHAN
Gardés vous de guerre et de noyse;
Ne forcés nulz, soyés crainctis!
172 Ne preignés riens oultre vous gages,
Et vivés counme vous Juïfz.

NYCODEMUS *ad Josept* 5a
Et puis, que vous en senble, sire Josept?

JOSEPH
C'est ung seint homme.

JACOB
Voyre, et parfait
176 Prophete cellon qu'il me senble.

PHINEAS AND LAZAY, *together to Saint John*
What must we do to remove our sin?
Tell us, master.

SAINT JOHN
What must you do?
164 If you have two coats, you must give one to the poor,
And also a portion of your other goods.

ZERAS AND JACOB *to Saint John*
Alas, and what shall we others do,
We public sinners?

SAINT JOHN
Nothing more, friends,
168 But painful penance.

JOSEPH *to Saint John*
And we of the gentry and nobility?

SAINT JOHN
Avoid wars and quarrels;
Use no force, be fearful.
172 Take nothing beyond your rightful wage,
And live like your Jews.

NICODEMUS *to Joseph*
Well, what do you think of him, Sir Joseph?

JOSEPH
He is a holy man.

JACOB
Truly he is, and a perfect
176 Prophet, as I think.

ZERAS
Je tranble
Car il m'a dit toute ma vie.

FINES
Je vous prie
180 Que soions tous baptizés.

LAZAY
Advisés,
Mes seigneurs, quelle voye prendrons.

JOSEPT
Advanssons!
184 Il est bon de nous baptiser.

(Tunc vadant ad Johannem.)

Pausa.

NYCODEMUS
Veullés nous baptesme donner,
Raby, pour vivre a honneur?

S. JEHAN
Dieu soit loué que voustre ceur
188 A esmeu pour vous fere esmender!
Sus, amys! Il vous fault despouller
Ycy pres du fleuve Jordain.

(Silete.)

Ce pendent que Jhesus parle Josept et ses conpaignons se despollent.

JHESUS *a genoulx voulant venir de Nazaret a seint Jehan baptiste*
Treshaut Dieu, pere souverein,
192 Don't j'ay ma divine substance
En essance,
Puis qu'il t'a pleu que soye humein,
Nourri de pein,
196 Je veulx faire ung peu d'abstinence

ZERAS
I am trembling
Because he has exposed my whole life.

PHINEAS
I beg you,
180 Let us all be baptized.

LAZAY
Tell me,
My lords, what path shall we take?

JOSEPH
Let us go forward.
184 It is right that we be baptized.

(Then let them go to John.)

Pausa.

NICODEMUS
Will you baptize us, Rabbi,
That we may live in honor?

SAINT JOHN
May God be praised, that he has moved your hearts
188 To make you amend your ways!
Get up, friends! You must take off your clothes
Here, near the river Jordan.

(Silete.)

While Jesus speaks, Joseph and his companions take off their clothes.

JESUS, *kneeling, wishing to come from Nazareth to Saint John the Baptist*
Most high God, sovereign father,
192 From whom I derive my divine substance
In essence,
Since it has pleased you that I take on human form,
Nourished by bread,
196 I wish to practice abstinence

Pour moustrer virtueuse senblence
De penictence
Entre les pouvres pecheurs,
200 Les quieulx rechater je pence 5b
En doleance,
Et leur admeriter honneurs.

Je leur veux moustrer bonnes meurs
204 Et virtüeuse humilité
En verité,
Pour les esmouvoir a doleurs
Et a pleurs
208 De leur mal et iniquité.
Je vaix droit sans obliquité
En equité
Prandre baptesme pour moustrer
212 Que lavement et mundicité
Et purté
Autres biens douevent preceder.

Avant que je voyse jeuner
216 Au desert ma grant quaranteine,
Pour estreine,
Les eaux veulx toutes sanctiffier
Et nectier,
220 Pour en faire doulce fonteine
De tout bien en grace pleine,
Ou hemeine
Fragilicté pardon ara
224 De tous ces maux et vie veine;
Lors certeine
De paradis elle sera.

S. JEHAN
Anprés moy vient qui baptisera
228 En vertu du seint esperit.
Lors chescun grace recevra
Qui de cueur se fera petit.

To show the virtuous face
Of penitence
To the poor sinners
200 Whom I intend to redeem
Through my pain,
And make them worthy of honor.

I wish to show them good habits
204 And virtuous humility
In truth,
To move them to grief
And to tears
208 For their crimes and wickedness.
So I shall go directly, without delay,
In righteousness
To receive baptism, to show
212 That washing and cleanness
And purity
Must precede all other virtues.

Before I go to fast
216 In the desert for full forty days,
To begin with
I wish to sanctify and cleanse
The waters,
220 That they may be as a sweet fountain
Of all good and grace
Where human
Frailty may find pardon
224 For all its crimes and empty life;
Then will it be assured
Of paradise.

SAINT JOHN
After me comes one who will baptize
228 By the power of the holy spirit.
Then all shall receive grace
Who in their hearts shall humble themselves.

NYCODEMUS
Raby, sans faire long respit,
232 Baptisés nous, je vous supplie.

S. JEHAN *ponendo aquam supra eos (dicat)*
(Tunc judicamur.)
Au nom du saulveur vous baptise
Qui doit venir sans plus actandre. *(Cilete.)*

Pausa. JHESUS
De ma mere veulx congié prandre,
236 Affin qu'elle soit consoulee.
Vadat ad Mariam matrem suam.
Bonne mere treshonnouree, 6a
Je viens a vous pour dire adieu,
Car il faut que jeune
240 Ung peu de temps.

MARIE
Pres de trente ans
Avons, mon filz, esté ensenble.
Toutesfois, m'amour, il me senble
244 Que le temps ne m'a riens duré,
Contenplant voustre deÿté,
Que tant est doulce et savoureuse;
Pour ce suis je tousjours joyeuse
248 Quant suis de vous aconpaigniee.
Hee, mon filz, ma doulce brassee,
Vous me ferés ung grant plaisir
S'il vous pleisoit prandre loisir
252 De demeurer encores ung peu.

JHESUS
Ma mere, il me fault müer lieu
Pour aller ouÿr Jehan baptiste.

MARIE
Mon filz, je n'en sceray ja triste.
256 Retournés tost, je vous enprie!

NICODEMUS
Rabbi, do not delay,
232 Baptize us, I beseech you.

(Let) SAINT JOHN, *pouring water over them, (say)*
(Tunc judicamur.)
I baptize you in the name of the Savior,
Who shall come without further delay. *(Cilete.)*
Pausa. JESUS
I must take leave of my mother,
236 That she may be consoled.
Let him go to Mary, his mother.
Most honored mother,
I come to you to say goodbye,
For I must fast
240 For a little while.

MARY
For nearly thirty years,
My son, we have been together.
However, to me, my love,
244 The time has not seemed very long,
Beholding your deity,
Which is so sweet and lovely;
For this am I always joyful,
248 When I am in your company.
Alas, my son, my sweet darling,
You will give me great pleasure
If you would kindly take leave
252 To stay with me a little longer.

JESUS
My mother, I must quit this place
To go to hear John the Baptist.

MARY
My son, I will not be sad on this account.
256 Return soon, I beg you!

JHESUS
Adieu, ma mere, m'amye.

MARIE
Adieu, mon filz.

JHESUS
Adieu, ma mere.

Pausa. *Tunc recedat Jhesus et Maria loquatur.*

MARIE
Mon crehateur, mon Dieu, mon pere,
260 En qui j'ay toute ma fïance
Et esperance,
A voustre grace me vaix traire
Et retrayre,
264 Affin qu'ayés en souvenance
Jhesus qui est de voustre essance,
Ma pleisance.
Pleise vous le moy retourner.
268 Certes, c'est toute ma chevance,
Ou je pansse
Mon corps et mon ame donner.

Pausa.

JHESUS 6b
Il est temps de m'abandonner
272 Pour conplir mon pellerinage.

Pausa.

Dieu vous sault, prophete tressaige,
Chivalier de Dieu tout puissant!

S. JEHAN
Et vous, sire, pareillement.
276 Vous plait il riens moy conmander?

JHESUS
Ouÿ. Velle moy baptiser!

S. JEHAN
Baptiser?

JESUS
Farewell, my mother, my love.

MARY
Farewell, my son.

JESUS
Farewell, my mother.

Pausa. *Then let Jesus withdraw and let Mary speak.*

MARY
My creator, my God, my father,
260 In whom is all my faith
And hope,
On your grace shall I call
And call again,
264 That you may remember
Jesus, who is of your own being,
And my pleasure.
Please return him to me.
268 Truly, he is my only love,
To whom I devote
My body and my soul.

Pausa.

JESUS
It is time for me to devote myself
272 To the fulfillment of my pilgrimage.

Pausa.

God save you, wise prophet,
Knight of almighty God!

SAINT JOHN
And you, sir, the same.
276 Do you wish anything of me?

JESUS
Yes. Baptize me, if you will!

SAINT JOHN
Baptize you?

Las, sauveur, et que dictes vous?
280 Je dois de vous baptesme prandre.
En riens ne vous vouldroie offendre,
Qui venés pour nous sauver tous.

JHESUS
Bon chivalier, leissés ses moutz.
284 Aconplir nous faut meinctenent
Entre nous deux treshunblement
Toute justice virtüeuse.

S. JEHAN
O saincte cher precïeuse,
288 Toucher je ne vous ouseroye.
Tout nut faut, seigneur, que vous voye
Pour conmencer nouvelle loy.

Pausa. *Expoliet se Jhesus.* (*Tunc descendat colunba prope Jhesus.*)

JHESUS
Je suis tout nu; baptise moy
292 Sans faire nul autre reffus.

S. JEHAN *ponendo aquam* (*dicat alta voce*)
Sanctiffïés moy, bon Jhesus,
Sanctiffïés moy, mon sauveur!

JHESUS
Ung sacrement de grant valleur
296 Meinctenent orne seincte eglise,
Quar ton seinct baptesme je prise,
Que circunsision ara fin
Et sera mon baptesme si fin
300 Que chescun y sera saulvé.

Tunc induat se Jhesus.

DIEU LE PERE *es anges* 7a
Illec est mon filz bien amé,
Qui a conmancé le baptesme.
Il a circunsision finé.

Oh, my Savior, what do you speak?
280 I should receive baptism from you.
I would not do you any offence,
You who come to save us all.

JESUS
Good knight, do not speak such words.
284 We must now, between us,
Humbly fulfill
All righteousness.

SAINT JOHN
Oh, precious, holy flesh,
288 I would not dare to touch you.
Naked must I see you, my Lord,
To begin the New Law.

Pausa. *Jesus disrobes. (Then let the dove descend near Jesus.)*

JESUS
Now I am naked; baptize me
292 Without further protest.

(Let) SAINT JOHN, *pouring the water, (say in a loud voice)*
Sanctify me, good Jesus,
Sanctify me, my savior!

JESUS
A sacrament of great worth
296 Now adorns our holy church,
For I value your holy baptism,
Which shall put an end to circumcision
And my baptism will be so perfect
300 That all men will be saved by it.

Then let Jesus put on his clothes.

GOD THE FATHER *to his angels*
This is my beloved son
Who has initiated baptism.
He has ended circumcision.

304 Il m'est pleisant; certes, je l'eyme.
Se qu'il fait m'est doulx counme cresme.
Il me plait eternellement.

Pausa modica.

O mes enfans, qu'estes son proheme,
308 Allés le louer doulcement!

GABRIEL

Nous y allons tout meinctenent,
Car joye nous y adresse.

Cum angellis colunba descendat et descendendo cantent id quod sequitur dulci cantu.

Chantons en grant liesse
312 A Jhesus le saulveur,
Quar Dieu par sa largesse
Es homes fait honneur,
Veu qu'ad eux nous adresse.
316 Loués* le redempteur (MS louer)
Qui pour sa grant prohesse
Sera noustre seigneur!

Alia copula.

O filz de Dieu le pere,
320 Filz de Dieu inmortel,
Au monde as* pris mere (MS a)
Pour te fere mortel.
Tu es en hault repaire,
324 Filz de Dieu eternel,
Conbien que ycy en terre
Soyes homme charnel.

S. JEHAN

O roy du ciel,
328 Prince des anges,
Oncques chant tiel
Ne tieulx louhanges
N'ay ouÿ entre les humeins.

304 He pleases me and surely I love him.
What he has done is as sweet to me as cream.
He pleases me ever.

Pausa modica.

My children, you who are his heralds,
308 Go praise him sweetly!

GABRIEL

We go, immediately,
For joy urges us on.

Let a dove descend with the angels and while they descend let them sing the following in a sweet song.

Let us sing in great joy
312 To Jesus our Savior,
For God in his bounty
Does honor to men,
Since he sends us to them.
316 Praise the redeemer
Who through his great prowess
Will become our lord.

Another verse.

O son of God the Father,
320 Son of the immortal God,
In the world you have chosen a mother
To make you mortal.
On high is your home,
324 Son of eternal God,
Although here on earth
You are a mortal man.

SAINT JOHN

O king of heaven,
328 Prince of angels,
Never such a song
Nor such praises
Have I heard on earth.

332 Chouses estranges
Sont a mes yeulx,
Colunbes blanches
Voulant des cieulx,
336 Dont je cognois le seint des seintz.

(Tunc surgit Johannis.)

Dieu gloriëux,
A qui je croy,
Pour avoir mieulx,
340 Baptisés moy
Tout meinctenent, je vous en prie.

JHESUS 7b
Despolle toy,
Je le veulx bien,
344 Affin que foy
Aie entrectien
En saincte eglise, m'ayme. *(Tunc angeli recedunt ad paradisum cantando.)*

S. JEHAN *en soy despollant*
Tout ne m'est rien
348 Fors que toy, mon Dieu;
Du tout suis tien
Et en tout lieu.
Veez me ycy, ton pouvre servent.

Pausa modica.

JHESUS
352 Je prens ton fieuf;
Il est tresbon.
L'eau de ce rieuf
Et mon seint nom
356 Sont ton baptesme et lavement;
Pour ce, mon amy, meinctenent
Au nom mon pere te baptise
Et de moy en terre vivant
360 Et de noustre esperit gracieulx.

332 Strange things
Do I see—
White doves
Flying down from the sky,
336 In which sight I recognize the holy of holies.

(Then John rises.)

Glorious God,
In whom I believe,
So that I may be more worthy,
340 Baptize me
Right away, I pray you.

JESUS
Undress yourself,
I will gladly do it,
344 So that faith
May be preserved
In the holy church, my spouse. *(Then the angels go back to Paradise, singing.)*

SAINT JOHN, *undressing*
All is nought to me,
348 Except you, my God;
I am yours in everything
And everywhere.
See me here, your poor servant.

Pausa modica.

JESUS
352 I accept your loyalty;
It is perfect.
The water of this river
And my holy name
356 Are your baptism and your cleansing;
I now baptize you, my friend,
In the name of my father,
And of me, living on earth,
360 And of our gracious spirit.

S. JEHAN
Jhesus, Dieu, homme glorïeux,
Je vous rans graces et mercy.

JHESUS
Adieu, prophete virtüeux.

S. ANDRIEU
364 Jhesus, Dieu, homme glorïeux!

SAMUEL
Veez cy mistere precïeux;
Certes, il fait tresbon ycy.

NATANAEL
Adieu, homme glorïeux!

S. JEHAN
368 Je vous rans graces et mercy. *Tunc induat se et Jhesus recedens dicit verba que sequntur.*

Pausa. JHESUS
Adonaÿ,
Mon Dieu, mon pere,
L'amour de ty,
372 Pour toy conplaire,
M'esmeut de m'aler mectre a part.
Pour mieulx attraire
L'umain lignage
376 Bon exanplere
Luy donrré je
De penictence en ce desert.
A celle part 8a
380 Par ceste voye
Vaix en escart,
Qu'on ne me voye,
Ou je veux quarante jours jeuner,
384 Affin qu'on croye

SAINT JOHN
Jesus, lord, glorious man,
I give you thanks.

JESUS
Farewell, virtuous prophet.

SAINT ANDREW
364 Jesus, lord, glorious man!

SAMUEL
Behold this precious mystery;
Surely wondrous things are happening here.

NATHANIEL
Farewell, glorious man!

SAINT JOHN
368 I give you thanks.

Then let him put his clothes on, and Jesus, retiring, speaks the words that follow.

Pausa.

JESUS
Adonai,
My God, my father,
My love for you,
372 That I may please you,
Leads me to withdraw apart.
To better lead
The human race,
376 I shall give it
A good example
Of penance in this desert.
To this region
380 By this path,
I go into the wilderness
So that no one may see me,
Where I will fast for forty days,
384 That men may believe

Que ton filz suis
Et qu'on oÿe
Mes motz et ditz.
388 Dieu, homme, je me veulx moustrer.

Agenoller
Ycy me fault
Pour contanpler
392 Mon pere en hault
Ad converser lamont es cieulx.
Soit froit ou chaut,
Quoy que m'adviegne,
396 Il ne m'en chaut,
Mais que je tiengne
En se desert la sus mes yeulx;
Car aussi sceray gloriëux
400 D'esperit en ma quaranteine,
Conbien que mon corps seuffre peine
De froit, de chaut ou de jeuner.

Remanet in deserto.

Pausa cum cillete modico.

HERODES
Mallifferas, il te fault aller
404 Querir Annas et Caÿphas.

MALIFERAS Cursor Herodis
Volantiers, sire; je feray grans pas.
Il ne fault guyeres demeurer.

MALIFFERAS *loquitur Anne et Cayphe.*
Mes seigneurs, Dieu vous veulle donner
408 Longue vie sans nul ennuy.

CAYPHAS* (MS Caphas)
Bien soiés venu, mon amy;
Quelles nouvelles?

I am your son
And that they may listen
To my words and sayings.
388 God and man I wish to show myself.

On my knees
Here must I be,
To contemplate
392 My father on high,
And to be with Him who is in heaven.
Be it cold or hot,
Whatever happens to me,
396 It will not matter,
Provided that I hold my gaze
Above in this desert.
For in this way I shall be glorious in spirit
400 During my forty days,
Although my body suffer pain
From cold or heat or fasting.

He remains in the desert.

Pausa cum cillete modico.

HEROD
Malifferas, you must go
404 And fetch Annas and Caiaphas.

MALIFFERAS, Herod's Messenger
Gladly, sire; I go with speed;
I must not delay even briefly.

MALIFFERAS *speaks with Annas and Caiaphas*
My lords, may God grant you
408 Long life with no harm.

CAIAPHAS
Welcome, my friend—
What news?

MALIFFERAS
Bonnes et belles!
412 C'est Herode qui vous demande
Et gracïeusement vous mande
Qu'ad luy vegniés diligement.

ANNAS
Nous y allons tout meinctenent.
416 Or allons tous!

Nator premier pharisien eundo dicat ad socios suos.

NATOR — 8b
Que panssés vous
Sur ce que Herodes vous demande?

BERIT Segont Farisieu
Je cuide que c'est pour la rante
420 Que Sesar veult de nous avoir.

CAYPHAS* — (MS Caphas)
Pas n'est possible de sçavoir
La bonne voulanté du roy.

ANNAS
Malifferas, advance toy;
424 Dy au roy que sommes venus.

MALIFFERAS
J'ay tant couru que n'en puis plus.
Pausa. Sire, vous gens sont a la voye.

HERODES
Je vays a eulx.

ANNAS ET CAIPHAS *ad Herodem loquntur in simul*

MALIFFERAS
Fair and good news.
412 It is Herod who calls you
And graciously bids you
Come quickly to him.

ANNAS
We are coming straightaway.
416 Come, let us all go.

Let Natort, the first Pharisee, speak to his companions as he goes.

NATORT
What do you think
Herod wants with us?

BERITH, The Second Pharisee
I think it is about the tax
420 That Caesar wants from us.

CAIAPHAS
We cannot know
What the gracious king wants.

ANNAS
Maliferas, go ahead;
424 Tell the king we are here.

MALIFFERAS
I have run so fast that I cannot move another step.
Pausa. Your men are on the way, sire.

HEROD
I shall go to them.

ANNAS AND CAIAPHAS *speak to Herod together*

Dieu vous doint joye!
428 Cher seigneur, qu'est se que vous plait?

HERODES
Amys, pour ce que nouveau fait,
Quant il est grant et mervilleus,
Affin qu'on y pourvoye mieulx,
432 Requiert conseill a peu de plait.
Il est vray q'un homme parfait,
Lequel se nomme Jehan baptiste,
Presche fort et se dit ministre
436 Et prophete tramis de Dieu.
Je ne sçay si avés nul lieu
Entre vous seinctes escriptures
En prophecies ou figures,
440 Que de luy fassent memoyre.

CAYPHAS
Voyre, dea, voyre,
Quar au Pentatequon Dieu promet
Q'un prophecte grant et parfait
444 Doit yssir de noustre ligniee.

HERODES
Et puis?

ANNAS
En unne autre contree
Hellïas, certes, nous promis.

NATORT 9a
Et Jacob entre ces beaulx ditz,
448 Parlant a son filz Juda,
Seurement il denunça
Ung redempteur devoir venir.

BERIT
Il me cuide bien souvenir
452 Qu'il a trante ans ou environ

God grant you joy!
428 Dear lord, what do you want?

HEROD
Friends, it is because a new event,
When it is great and miraculous,
Requires instant attention
432 If one is to deal with it properly.
The truth is that a man without sin,
Who is called John the Baptist,
Preaches much and claims to be a minister
436 And prophet sent by God.
I would like to know if there is any place
In your holy scriptures,
Either in prophesies or figures,
440 Which mentions him.

CAIAPHAS
Yes, by God, there is,
For in the Pentateuch God promises
That a mighty and sinless prophet
444 Shall issue from our line.

HEROD
What more?

ANNAS
In a different country
Elijah, certainly, has promised us the same.

NATORT
And Jacob, too, among his fine sayings,
448 Speaking to his son Judah,
Announced, without doubt,
That a redeemer should come.

BERITH
I think I remember
452 That about thirty years ago or so

Q'un prebstre de bien grant renon
Qu'on appelloit Jacaret,
Et sa famme de bonne vie,
456 Heurent en leur viellesse ung filz,
Dont nous fusmes tous esbaÿs,
Et furent chouses mervilleuses
Lors dites et miraculeuses,
460 Tant du filz counme des parens.

HERODES
Certes, c'est tout le bruyt des gens;
Et m'a on dit que c'est celluy
Et ne parlet on que de luy.
464 Advisés doncques. Qu'est de faire?

CAYPHAS
Se n'est pas ung petit affaire.
Il y fault tresbien adviser.

ANNAS
Grandement le fauldroit priser,
468 Si s'estoit le prophecte grant.

NATORT
Et s'il estoit ung truhant,
Il le fauldroit faire cesser.

HERODES
Or doncques, sans plus diviser,
472 Envoyons sçavoir de son cas.

CAYPHAS ET ANNAS
C'est tresbien dit.

HERODES
Malifferas,
Dilligenment et sans respit,

A priest of great renown,
Named Zachariah,
And his wife of virtuous life,
456 Had a son in their old age,
At which we were all astonished,
And wondrous things were
Then said, marvelous things,
460 Both about the son and about his parents.

HEROD
Indeed, everyone is talking about it;
And I have been told that he is the one
And no one speaks of anything else but him.
464 Tell me then, what is to be done?

CAIAPHAS
This is no minor matter.
We must consult well.

ANNAS
If he were indeed the great prophet,
468 We would have to revere him greatly.

NATORT
And if he were an impostor,
We would have to put an end to him.

HEROD
Now, then, without further dispute,
472 Let us send somebody to seek out the truth about him.

CAIAPHAS AND ANNAS
That is a very good idea.

HEROD
Malifferas,
And you too, Natort and Berith,

Vous trois, Natort et Berit,
476 Dilligenment a luy yrés;
De par moy luy demanderés
Qu'il est. Reportés sans mantir.

MALIFFERAS 9b
De tresbon cueur veulx aconplir
480 Voustre voulouyr, trescher sire.

NATORT ET BERIT
Adieu, seigneurs.

CAYPHAS
Sans plus dire,
Allés et faictes bon devoir.

S. JEHAN *a ces disciples et autres*
Sachés, mes bons amys, pour veoir,
484 Qu'ad Dieu sommes fort obligés,
Car pour nous ouster nous pechés
Par sa charité souvereine,
A mys son filz en cher humeine
488 A souffrir peine et tourment.
Il croistra en peine souffrant,
Et en mourant je viendré moindre.

MALIFFERAS *a ses conpaignons*
Mes seigneurs, il ne fault nul creindre;
492 Parlés a luy, car il est tart.

NATORT *a seint Jehan*
Raby, Dieu vous doint bonne part
De se que desirés le plus!

S. JEHAN
Mes amys, bien soyés venus!
496 Est il riens que veullés de moy?

All three of you go to him
476 Quickly and without delay.
In my name, ask him
Who he is. Bring me back his answer, without lies.

MALIFFERAS
I am willing, honored sire,
480 Most gladly to accomplish your will.

NATORT AND BERITH
Farewell, my lords.

CAIAPHAS
Without further ado,
Go and do your duty.

SAINT JOHN, *to his disciples and others*
Know, my good friends, in truth,
484 That we owe a debt to God,
For in order to remove our sins from us,
Through his sovereign charity
He has sent his son, in human flesh,
488 To suffer pain and torment.
He shall grow great in suffering pain,
And I, in dying, shall become less.

MALIFFERAS *to his companions*
My lords, we have no one to fear;
492 Speak to him, for it is getting late.

NATORT *to Saint John*
Rabbi, may God grant you a good share
Of what you most desire!

SAINT JOHN
My friends, you are welcome.
496 Is there anything you wish from me?

BERIT
Nous sommes cy tramis du roy
Et de par les princes du tenple
Pour avoir de toy cognoissance,
500 Si tu es Crist. Dy le nous,
Et leur raporterons tes motz.
Et si non, dy nous qui tu es!

S. JEHAN
A brief parler, sans faire excés,
504 Seurement Crist ne suis je pas.

MALIFFERAS
Quoy, doncques, es tu Hellïas?
Or dy!

S. JEHAN
Nany!

NATORT 10a
508 Nany?
Quoy, doncques, es tu prophete?

S. JEHAN
Non!

BERIT
Non?
512 Non est pas responce parfaicte
Pour rapporter a nous seigneurs.
Dy nous de toy cellon tes meurs,
Qui tu es, pour response randre,
516 Pour nous garder de mesprandre* (MS mespandre)
A ceulx qui a toy nous ont tramys.

S. JEHAN
Freres, je suis *vox clamantis*
Dans le desert, affin qu'on m'oye,

BERITH
We have been sent here by the king
And on behalf of the princes of the temple
To find out from you
500 If you are the Christ. Tell us,
And we shall report your words to them.
And if you are not he, tell us who you are!

SAINT JOHN
To speak briefly, without many words,
504 I assure you, I am not the Christ.

MALIFFERAS
Well, then, are you Elijah?
Speak!

SAINT JOHN
Nay!

NATORT
508 Nay?
Well, then, are you a prophet?

SAINT JOHN
No!

BERITH
No?
512 "No" is not an adequate reply
To report to our lords.
Tell us about yourself, about your way of life,
And who you are, that we may give a reply
516 That will keep us from misleading
Those who have sent us to you.

SAINT JOHN
Brothers, I am the *vox clamantis*
In the wilderness, that men may hear me,

520 Disant que preparés la voye
A noustre seigneur Messïas.
De moy parlast Ysaÿas
En son quarantiesme chappitre.

MALIFFERAS
524 Doncques, si tu n'as aultre tiltre,
Qui te fait les gens baptiser?

S. JEHAN
Je ne fais que les corps laver.
Mes entre vous est ung moyen,
528 Le quel ne cognoiscés en rien.
Il est tropt plus parfait que moy;
Il viendra prescher la foy,
Qui devant moy a esté fait;
532 Et pour abresger tout se plaist,
Je ne suis pas digne de deslier
Les corroyes de son sollier,
Tant est de grace ranplit.

NATORT
536 Il nous souffit.

BERIT
Adieu, raby!

Pausa.
Allons nous en droit noustre voye;
Il nous faut avanser nous pas.

Pausa.
Que t'en senble, Malifferas?
540 N'est se pas ung homme de bien?

MALIFFERAS 10b
Tu ne le ressanbles en rien.
Il dit qu'il en est ung melleur,
Le quel sera noustre seigneur.

520 Telling you to prepare the way
For our Lord, the Messiah.
Of me did Isaiah speak
In his fortieth chapter.

MALIFFERAS
524 Well, then, if you have no other title,
Who is making you baptize people?

SAINT JOHN
I do nothing but cleanse their bodies.
But among you is an agent of the Lord
528 Whom you do not know at all.
He is much more powerful than I;
He will come to preach the faith,
He who was made before me;
532 And briefly to end this conversation,
I am not worthy to untie
The straps of his sandal,
So full of grace is he.

NATORT
536 That is enough for us.

BERITH
Farewell, Rabbi!

Pausa.

Let us go straight on our way.
We must hasten on our journey.

Pausa.

What do you think of him, Malifferas,
540 Is he not a good man?

MALIFFERAS
You do not resemble him at all.
He says that there is a better man than he,
Who shall be our Lord.

544 C'est chouse que ne puis croire.
J'ay grant soif. Je vouldroye boyre.

Pausa modica.

Allons parler a nos seigneurs.

MALIFFERAS
Dieu vous doint le tronne d'onneur,
548 Sire roy, et a la conpaignie!

HERODE
Et puis?

NATORT
Noustre messaigerie
Nous avons fait tresseurement.
Se prophete dit vraiement
552 Que il n'est Crist ne Hellie,
Et aussi que prophete n'est mye,
Mes que il baptise en eau.

CAYPHE
Quel homme est il?

BERIT
Pellu coumme ung vehau,
556 Et vestu d'ung fort rude drapt
Qu'a si a la fasson d'ung sac,
Pres nutz, maigre counme ung hours.

ANNAS
Et puis?

MALIFFERAS
Il dit qu'il est *vox*
560 Que prophetisast Ysaÿe
En sa predication. Il crie
Q'un p. s grant que luy doit venir.

544 That is something I cannot believe.
I'm thirsty, I want a drink.

Pausa modica.

Now let us go speak to our lords.

MALIFFERAS

God grant you the throne of glory,
548 Sir king, and all your company!

HEROD

Well?

NATORT

We have accomplished
Our mission, without fail.
This prophet swears
552 That he is neither Christ nor Elijah,
Nor is he a prophet,
But baptizes with water.

CAIAPHAS

What sort of man is he?

BERITH

Hairy as a calf,
556 Clothed in a very crude robe
Which he wears like a sack,
Almost naked, lean as a bear.

ANNAS

What else?

MALIFFERAS

He says that he is the *vox*
560 That Isaiah prophesied
In his sermon. He announces
That one greater than he is to come.

HERODES
Or sa, il le me fault ouÿr
564 Unne fois en toute ma vie.

Pausa cum cilete.

LUCIFER 11a
Haro! Haro! Sus, dyablerie!
Sathan, Belzebut, Astarot,
Laissés sabin, sabat, sabaut,
568 Pour escouter ma crïerie.

SATHAN
Enfer, maldicte soit t'envye!
Qu'as tu trouvé, dy, Cerberus?

LUCIFER
Haro, se prophete Jhesus
572 Au desert fait grant penictence,
Voire plus grande qu'autres nulz,
Encores plus.
Il semble qu'il aye toute science
576 Et ignoscence
Et la puissance de lassus.
Jehan baptiste tout confus
A fait refus.
580 Le baptiser n'a pas long temps,
Et lors entre eulx ont conclus
Que Jhesus
Sanctiffïeroit toutes gens.

SATHAN
584 Mauldit enfer, estrainct tes dens,
Augmente ta fureur et malice
Et ton vice,
Ou tu perdras tous tes enfans,
588 Eux nians,
Et lors seras reputé nyce,
Quant tu verras ronpre tes liens
Estraignans,

HEROD
Well, then, I must hear him
564 At least once in my life.

Pausa cum cilete.

LUCIFER
Haro, haro! Arise, devils!
Satan, Beelzebub, Ashtaroth,
Up with you, quit your black sabbaths,
568 Listen to my cries.

SATAN
A pox on your shouting, King of Hell.
What have you found, Cerberus, tell us?

LUCIFER
Haro! This prophet Jesus
572 Is in the desert doing penance
Greater, in truth, than any other
Has ever done.
He seems to have all wisdom
576 And innocence
And heavenly power.
John the Baptist, in awe of him,
Refused to baptize him.
580 But the baptism did not take long,
And now between them they have decided
That Jesus
Should sanctify the human race.

SATAN
584 Accursed Hell, clench your teeth,
Let your evil, wrath, and malice
Grow,
Or you shall lose all your children,
588 Rejecting them,
And then what a fine reputation you will have,
When you see your taut chains
Broken asunder,

592 Et ne prendras plus nulle proye.
Mieulx te vauldroit* pardre ton sens (MS vouldroit)
Enragens.
Or doncques a mal nous enploye!

LUCIFER

596 Je n'y sçay plus chemin ne voye
Ne cauthelle que soit propice.

SATHAN

O Lucifer, prince de vice,
Et vous, dyables, de Dieu haïs,
600 Escoutés ma voix et mes critz!
Long temps a que par ma cauthelle
J'acquis celle nature belle 11b
Des hommes malicieusement
604 Et la demenys tellement
Que non obstant qu'elle fut creee* (MS cree)
Pour estre en paradis lougee,
Aux sieges dont chumes sa bas,
608 Toutesfois pour mes entrepas
Elle a pardu du ciel la voye
Et est meinctenent noustre proye.
Je vous dy tout secy pour tant
612 Que si nous mectons peine grant
A tempter ce prophete Jhesus,
Je croy que tost sceras confus
Et le tirerons ad nous liens.

BELZEBUT

616 Il vault mieulx y mectre vint ans
A le tempter;
Nous ne pouvons que peine perdre.

ASTAROT

Haro, que mal feu d'enfer vous arde!
620 Pour en taster
Nous n'y pardrons ja noustre peine.

592 And when you no longer capture any victims.
Better that you should waste your senses
In rage.
Now, set us an evil task.

LUCIFER

596 I don't know what route or path
Or cunning is best for us.

SATAN

O Lucifer, prince of evil,
And you, devils, hated of God,
600 Listen to my voice and my words!
Long ago did I gain control
Of mankind's noble nature
Through my wiles,
604 And I mistreated him so that
Even though he was created
To be lodged in paradise,
In those very seats from which we fell so low,
608 Nevertheless, entirely through my trickery,
Did he lose the way to heaven,
And he is now our prey.
I tell you this because
612 If we make a great effort
To tempt this prophet, Jesus,
I believe he will soon be destroyed
And we will drag him here to our prison.

BEELZEBUB

616 We could spend twenty years
Tempting him,
And we would still lose our pains.

ASHTAROTH

Haro! May you burn in the fires of hell!
620 In testing him
We will not lose our pains.

ASMO
Du feu d'enfer pour voustre estreine
Puissés bruller!
624 Alons a luy. Que doubtés vous?

SATHAN
Enrager puissés vous trestous
Et dessener;
Nous l'arons bien si y mectons cure.

ASMO
628 Mauldit enfer, donne moy procure!
En la conpaignie de Sathan
Tu ses bien que c'est ma nacture
De donner aux humeins mal an.

632 Je frappe, je tue, je discorde,
Je fais divisions et debas,
J'estrangle les gens par ma corde,
De lieu hault je les rue en bas.

636 Je feis que Caÿn tua son frere
Et que David par trahison
Urïas mist en tel reppaire
Qu'il morust sens cause et reyson.

SATAN
640 Et je feis qu'Absalon tua Amon 12a
Et que Jobil Amasian frappa;
Abmellec nul ne leissa
De ses freres pour avoir nom.

644 J'ay fait encores plus avant,
Car plus de cinq cens mille personnes
J'ay fait entrectuer pour neant
En guerres et autres grans foulles.

ASMO
648 Je mes le feu a froides coulles
Et les faitz luxurier a force;
Je fais manger grasses endoulles

ASMO
May you burn in hell
For your reward!
624 Let us go to him. What do you fear?

SATAN
May all of you go mad
And lose your senses.
We'll have him, all right, if we take care.

ASMO
628 Accursed Hell, give me a commission.
You know well that in Satan's company
It is my nature
To give human beings a bad time.

632 I hit them, I kill them, I set them at odds,
I sow dissension and discord,
I strangle men with my rope,
From high places I hurl them below.

636 It was I who made Cain kill his brother,
And I who made David,
Through treachery, put Uriah in such a spot
That he died, without cause or reason.

SATAN
640 And it was I who made Absalom kill Amnon,
And Joab strike Amasa;
Abimelech left not one of his brothers
Alive to bear his name.

644 I have done more than this,
For more than five hundred thousand people
Have I made kill each other, for nothing,
In wars and other great frays.

ASMO
648 I put the fire of lust in cold livers,
And make men burn with hot desire;
I make them eat greasy sausages

Et d'espices la chaude escorsse.

652 Je fais les hommes tous goullus
Et les fais bruler d'advarice.
Que voulés vous que fasse plus?
Je suis le tempteur en tout vice.

656 Et pour ce, dyables, je vous jure
Que nous arons bien se Jhesus,
Mais qu'il soit entre nous conclus
Qu'avec Satham j'aye procure.

LUXIFER

660 Mauldicte soit voustre nature!
Allés y; ne faictes demeure!

SATHAM

Tous deux y yrons a ceste heure,
Puis qu'ausi le nous conmandés.

ASTAROT

664 Premier vous fault avoir procure.

ASMO

Tous deux y yrons a ceste heure.

BELZEBUT

Premier vous fault avoir procure
Pour la fin ou vous pretancdés.

SATHAM

668 Tous deux y yrons a ceste heure,
Puis qu'aussi le nous consellés.

LUCIFER 12b

Actendés, dyables, actendés!
Pour mieulx faire vous peremptoires,
672 Veez cy lectres procuratoueres
Escriptes sur peaux de puteins
Et singnees de mes deux mains,

And the hot skins of spices.

652 I make men greedy
And set them on fire with avarice.
What more could you want?
I tempt men to every vice.

656 And therefore, devils, I promise you
We will get this Jesus.
Provided that we agree
That with Satan I have the commission.

LUCIFER
660 A curse upon you!
Get going; no more delay!

SATAN
The two of us are going right away,
Since you order us to do it.

ASHTAROTH
664 First you must have your commission.

ASMO
The two of us are going, right away.

BEELZEBUB
First you must have your commission
For the goal that you intend.

SATAN
668 The two of us are going right away,
Since you order us to do it.

LUCIFER
Wait, devils, wait!
To help you better carry out your mission,
672 Here are your letters of commission
Written on the skins of whores,
And signed by both my hands,

Au papier d'enfer enregistrees,
676 De souffre et de poye scelees,
Donnees en noustre parlement
Et devant tous publicquement.
Allés tost! Faictez dilligence;
680 Tenés vous lectres de creance
Et voustre procuratïon.

SATHAN
Luxifer, ta malediction
Donne nous pour mieulx besongnier!

LUXIFER
684 Allés en grant tribulation!

ASMO
Luxifer, ta malediction!

LUXIFER
Allés en grant tribulation!
De Dieu puissés vous allongner!

SATHAN
688 Luxifer, ta malediction
Donne nous pour mieulx besongner!

LUXIFER
Ou feu d'enfer puissés baigner
Dedans les chaudieres boullans!
692 Soiés a mal fere vallans!
Gardés vous de venir sans proye!
De ma puissance vous octroye
Inffinie pugnitïon
696 Et aprés maledictïon,
Sans jamais avoir bien ne joye.

ASMO
Accopt, Sathan! Allons noustre voye.
Dilligenment advanssons nous!

On paper registered in hell,
676 Sealed with sulphur and pitch,
Issued here in our parliament
Publicly before all.
Go quickly! Make haste!
680 Take your letters of authorization
And your commission.

SATAN
Lucifer, give us your curse,
That we may better perform this deed!

LUCIFER
684 Go forth in tribulation!

ASMO
Lucifer, give us your curse!

LUCIFER
Go forth in tribulation!
May you keep well away from God!

SATAN
688 Lucifer, give us your curse,
That we may better perform this deed!

LUCIFER
May you bathe in hell-fire
In boiling cauldrons!
692 May you be valiant in evil!
May you be careful not to return without a prize!
Through my power I grant you
The right to infinite punishment
696 And, after, curses
Without ever tasting happiness or joy.

ASMO
Quickly, Satan! Let us go our way,
Obediently let us be off!

Pausa cum cillete.

Tunc surgit Jhesus et Sathan et Asmo appropincquant ad eum; videlicet Satham in veste heremite.

JHESUS 13a

700 Mon Dieu, mon pere tresdoulx,
Coumme tu sces, il faut que voise
Exaulcer ma voix et mes motz.
Je presupose qu'il te plaise.
704 Meinctenent faut que preigne noise
Contre Sathan, la cher et le monde.
Ja le jeune tropt fort me poise;
Par juner ma face est profunde.
708 Mon pere ou* tout bien habunde, (MS out)
Il me fault visicter la terre
D'Israel, qu'on ne la confunde
Par peché et mauvaise guerre.
712 Je voy que le dyable dessarre
Ses dartz de temptacïon.
Il veut bons et mauvaix acquerre
Et mectre a dampnatïon.
716 Mes par ma predicatïon
Bien le vouldroye confundre,
Mectre gens ad salvatïon
Et les pechés de tout estraincdre.
720 Au peuple d'Israel, qui craindre
Te vouldra, pere, m'as tramis,
Entre les quieulx me feray moindre,
Affin qu'en moy preignent advis.
724 Je vais conmencer mes preschis
En Nazaret droit ceste voye.

SATHAM

Mon bon raby, Dieu vous doint joye!

JHESUS

Voulantiers, las, je mangeroie,
728 Si* j'avoye ung peu de pein bis. (MS je)

Pausa cum cillete.

Then Jesus rises and Satan and Asmo approach him; namely, Satan disguised as a hermit.

JESUS

700 My lord, my most merciful father,
As you know, I must now go
To carry out my promise.
This, I know, is your will.
704 Now must I do battle
Against the world, the flesh, and the devil.
Already fasting is heavily wearing me down.
Through fasting is my face grown hollow.
708 My father, in whom all good abounds,
I must go to the land
Of Israel, that it may not be confounded
By sin and evil war.
712 I see that the devil is unloosing
His darts of temptation.
He wishes to seize both the righteous and the unrighteous,
And lead them to damnation.
716 But by my preaching
I hope to confound him,
Lead men to salvation,
And completely absolve all their sins.
720 To the people of Israel, who shall wish
To live in fear of you, you have sent me,
Among whom I shall make myself more humble
That they may heed my word.
724 I shall go along this path here
To begin my preaching in Nazareth.

SATAN

God give you joy, Rabbi!

JESUS

Gladly, alas, I would fain eat
728 If I had a piece of brown bread.

SATHAM
Si de Dieu es nacturel filz,
Bien pourras convertir en pein
Ses pierres que j'ay en ma main.
732 Counme toy, j'ay fein, je t'affie.
Or le fais donc, je t'en supplie,
Et entre nous deux mangerons.

JHESUS
Ne sces tu pas se que lisons
736 En noustre seincte escripture?
Seul pain n'est pas la norriture
De l'omme, se non pour le corps,
Quar l'ame qu'a meincts remortz 13b
740 Se nourrit du verbe divin
Et de tous ses sermons, affin
Que pour peché jamais ne meure.

SATHAN
Or sa, Jhesus, tout a ceste heure
744 Ma puissance te moustreré.
Sur le tenple te pourtaré
Pour toy faire plus grant honneur.

Tunc Satham portat Jhesum supra pinaculum templi et Jhesus loquitur.

JHESUS
On doit honnourer son seigneur
748 En quelque place qu'on le treuve;
Pour ce ne m'est nul disonneur
Si ta puissance je preuve.
Toutes fois il faut que je treuve
752 Le bien et le mal qu'est en moy,
A celle fin qu'on ne contreuve
Sur moy faulceté de la loy.

Tunc apparet Satham in specie sacerdotis et loquitur.

SATAN
If you are the natural son of God,
You can easily convert into bread
These stones which I hold in my hand.
732 Like you, I am hungry, I assure you.
Now, do it, I beg you,
And we shall both eat.

JESUS
Do you not know what we read
736 In our holy scripture?
"Bread alone is not the substenance
Of man, but only of his body,"
For the soul living in torment
740 Is nourished by the Divine Word
And by all its sermons, so that
It shall never die from sin.

SATAN
Now, Jesus, even at this very moment,
744 I shall show you my power.
To the top of the temple shall I carry you,
To do you greater honor

Then Satan carries Jesus to the pinnacle of the Temple, and Jesus says.

JESUS
One should honor one's lord
748 Wherever one finds him;
Therefore there is no dishonor to me
If I test your power.
I must still seek
752 The good and the evil that is in me,
To the end that no disobedience to the law
May be imagined in me.

Then Satan appears in the guise of a priest, and says.

SATHAN

Bien vouldroie congnoistre en toy
756 Si filz de Dieu es naturel,
Pour toy servir en bonne foy
Counme le vray Emanüel.
Escript est que Dieu eternel
760 A conmandé a tous ces anges
Que a toy, son filz celestïel,
Gardent de rancontres estranges.
Moustre tes biens et tes louanges,
764 Et te gecte d'ycy la bas,
Si ne te casses piés ne anches!
Lors filz de Dieu te moustreras,
Car des anges gardé sceras,
768 Aussi que David l'a escript;
Et des Juïfz louhange aras
Plus grant qu'oncques n'eust David!

JHESUS

Moÿse Penthatecon fist
772 Pour la loy de Dieu enseigner,
Auquel ceste doctrine mist:
Ton Dieu tu ne velles tempter.
Pour ce ne veulx pas actampter
776 Saulter la bas en esperance — 14a
Que mon Dieu me feroit aider
De ses anges par sa puissance.
Se seroit grant aultrecuidanse.
780 Car par alleurs dessendre puis
Assaier de Dieu la puissance;
Par aussi m'en voix par cest huis.

SATHAN

Haro, mauldit soit le partuis,
784 Ensemble celluy qui l'a fait!

ASMO

Il t'a ballé deux retreinctis,
Sathan, pour toy moustrer qu'il scet!

SATAN

I truly wish to know
756 If you are the natural son of God,
That I may serve you loyally
As the true Emmanuel.
It is written that eternal God
760 Has ordered all his angels
To protect you, his heavenly son,
From any misadventure.
Show your might and your glory
764 And throw yourself down from here,
Without breaking your feet and your legs.
Then shall you show that you are the son of God,
For you shall be protected by angels,
768 As David has written;
And you shall have praise from the Jews
Greater than any David had!

JESUS

Moses wrote the Pentateuch
772 To teach the law of God,
In which this doctrine is written:
"Thou shalt not tempt thy God."
Therefore I shall not attempt to
776 Jump down from here in the hope
That God will aid me
With his angels, through his power.
That would be a great presumption.
780 For I can descend otherwise
Than by testing God's power;
By a different way I shall go, through this gate.

SATAN

Haro! cursed be that opening,
784 And he who made it!

ASMO

He has dealt you two rebuffs,
Satan, to show you what he can do.

SATHAN
Il m'en desplait
788 A peu de plait;
Autrement le me faut assalir.

ASMO
Acconplir
Ton desir
792 Tu ne pourras; si me doubte.

SATHAN
Dans ma hocte
Lourde et socte
Le mectray pour le pourter hault.

ASMO
796 Il est cault
Par assault.
Sathan, tu ne l'aras mye!

SATHAN
Encore unne aultre assalie
800 De moy ara tout meinctenent.

Tunc portat Jhesum supra montem et Jhesus sequencia dicit.

JHESUS
O Dieu, mon pere tout puissant,
Tu veulx que me laisse porter
Pour donner example luisant
804 Es pecheurs a les conforter,
Affin qu'ilz puissent rapporter
Quelque fruit de ma resistence,
Et doresenavant suppourter
808 Mal, douleur et aultre grevance.

14b

SATHAM
Raby, j'ay unne grant chevansse,

Tunc apparet Satham in specie regis.

SATAN
To put it bluntly,
788 I am not at all pleased with him.
I will try a different tactic.

ASMO
You will not be able
To accomplish
792 Your wish, I think.

SATAN
In my hood,
Heavy and foolish,
Shall I put him to carry him above.

ASMO
796 He is clever
In the face of attack.
Satan, you will never get him!

SATAN
One more attack now
800 He'll get from me.

Then he takes Jesus on top of a mountain and Jesus speaks the following.

JESUS
O God, my omnipotent father,
It is your will that I let myself be borne here
To give a radiant example
804 To sinners, to comfort them,
That they may reap the fruit
Of my endurance,
And henceforth bear up against
808 Evil, pain, and other grief.

Then Satan appears in the likeness of a king.

SATAN
Rabbi, I have great wealth,

Et suis seigneur de grant païs:
Angleterre, Bourgonnhe et France,
812 Tout est mien! Et tous reaulmes juifz:
Perce, Babillouene et Tarcis;
Et se que pouvons regarder
Du monde soubz le ciel conpris
816 Tout te donrré, si me veulx adourer!

JHESUS
Va, mallereux en enffer!
Escoute que nous dit la seincte escripture:
Dieu, ton seigneur, te convient adourer,
820 Servir et honnourer par reison et droicture.
Car luy seul precede toute crehature,
Soit en se monde, en enffer ou en gloire.

SATHAM
Haro, haro, mauldicte soit ma cure!
824 Je n'ay riens fait. Las, du tout il me fault taire.
Vadant ad infernum.
ASMO
Mauldit Satham, fuons a mal reppaire,
Ou nous scerons, je cuide, bien gallés.

SATHAM
O Luxifer, nous sommes tous allés,
828 Et n'avons riens fait!

LUXIFER
Pour quoy?

ASMO
Quar tant est perfaict
Se prophecte Jhesus
Que tantost* cognoist (MS tanstot)
832 Nous cautelleux abus.

And am lord of a great country:
England, Burgundy and France,
812 All these are mine! all the Jewish kingdoms too:
Persia, Babylon, and Tarsus;
All that we can see from here
Of the earth beneath the heavens
816 Will I give you, if you will worship me!

JESUS
Go, wicked one, to hell-fire!
Listen to what the holy scriptures tell us:
You must love God, your lord,
820 And serve and honor him, through reason and right.
For he alone excels all creatures,
Whether in this world, in hell, or in heavenly glory.

SATAN
Haro, haro! Cursed be the pains that I have taken.
824 I have accomplished nothing. Alas, I must be silent evermore!

Let them go to Hell.

ASMO
Accursed Satan, let us flee to our evil abode,
Where we will, I think, be well entertained.

SATAN
O Lucifer, we have both made our journey,
828 But have accomplished nothing!

LUCIFER
Why?

ASMO
Because this prophet Jesus
Is so perfect
That he soon saw through
832 Our clever deceit.

LUXIFER
O dyables, frappés sus
A Asmo et a Satham;
De la dant Serberus
836 Mectés les en mal an!

ASTAROT *percutiendo Satham*
Tien cella, truhan;
Que mauldit soies tu!
Au feu Targnanam
840 Soies tu reffundu!

BELZEBUT *percutiendo Asmo loquitur* 15a
Tien, pallart goullu!
Tu aras ce tatin.
Tu sceras confundu
844 Du feu de Galgatin!

Pausa cum cilete.

MARIE
Souverein Dieu qui es sans fin,
Ung peu veulle moy consoler.
Envoye moy ad ce matin
848 Mon filz pour ung peu l'acouler.
Fors luy riens ne me peut souller,
Mon tresdoulx Dieu, coumme certes scavés.
Faictes qu'il aye de mon petit soupper
852 Que j'ay preparé, quar fere le poués.

DIEU LE PERE
Sus, Gabrïel, dilligenment allés,
Vous et Urïel, ensemble Raphael,
Droit ad Marie, que doulcement amés,
856 Et son soupper, ou elle mect du sel,
A mon enfant le doulx Emanüel
Pourtés ligier, car il a grant fain;
Et puis luy faictes service cordiel

LUCIFER
O devils, beat them,
Beat Asmo and Satan;
With the tooth of Cerberus
836 Put them to pain.

ASHTAROTH, *beating Satan*
Take that, you wretch;
A curse upon you!
In the Targnanian fire
840 May you be melted.

BEELZEBUB, *striking Asmo, says*
Take that, you knavish glutton!
You shall have some blows.
You shall be destroyed
844 By the fires of Galgatin!

Pausa cum cilete.

MARY
Lord God, eternal one,
Comfort me a little, if you will.
Send me this morning
848 My son, that I may embrace him briefly.
No one but he can satisfy me,
Most merciful God, as you surely know.
Grant that he may partake of the little supper
852 I have prepared, for it is in your power.

GOD THE FATHER
Arise, Gabriel, go quickly,
You and Uriel, and Raphael too,
To Mary without delay, whom you love so tenderly,
856 And take the meal on which she is sprinkling some salt
To my child, the sweet Emmanuel—
And take it quickly, for he is very hungry;
And then do him friendly service

860 Pour le descendre de son roch en lieu plain.

GABRIEL
Sans point de faulte, noustre roy souverein,
A celle part yrons dilligenment.

Tunc Deus pater tradit panem angellis et dicit hec verba sequencia.

DIEU LE PERE
Allés courant et luy pourtés ce pein.

RAPHAEL
864 Sans point de faulte, noustre roy souverein.

DIEU LE PERE
Chascun de vous le preigne par la main
Pour le descendre plus glorieusement.

GABRIEL
Sans point de faulte, noustre roy souverein,
868 A celle part yrons dilligenment.

Angelli descendendo cantent, Gabriel Raphael et Uriel portantes panem, in cantu comuni id quod sequitur dulciter.

ANGELLI *cantando dicunt* 15b
Du pain de gloire doulcement
A Dieu pourtons homme mortel,
Conbien qu'il soit le pein vivant,
872 Dieu gloriëux et inmortel.

RAPHAEL
Veés cy de Marie l'ostel.
Il fault que la saluons tous.

Dicant omnes.
Ave Maria!

860 To help him come down from that rock to the open plain.

GABRIEL
Without fail, our sovereign lord,
Shall we go there quickly.

Then God the Father gives bread to the angels and speaks the following words.

GOD THE FATHER
Go speedily, and bring him this bread.

RAPHAEL
864 Without fail, our sovereign lord.

GOD THE FATHER
Each of you, take him by the hand,
That he may descend in greater glory.

GABRIEL
Without fail, our sovereign lord,
868 Shall we go there quickly.

As they descend, Gabriel, Raphael and Uriel carrying the bread, let the angels sing sweetly, in chorus, that which follows.

THE ANGELS, *singing, say*
Let us gently take the bread of glory
To God, now mortal man,
Though he be the living bread,
872 Glorious and immortal God.

RAPHAEL
See, there is Mary's home.
We must all greet her together.

Let them all speak together.
Ave Maria!

MARIE

Mes amys doulx,

876 Vous sçoyés les tresbien venus!

Pausa.

Hellas, ou est mon filz Jhesus?
M'en pourtés vous point de nouvelles?

URIEL

Voere, dame.

MARIE

Quelles?

GABRIEL

Elles sont belles.

MARIE

880 Conment?

GABRIEL

Pour tant
Qu'il a fait unne grant vallance
Contre Sathan et sa puissance,
884 Et l'en a tramis tout confus.

MARIE

Quoy plus?

GABRIEL

Sachés, dame, que de la sus
Nous luy pourtons se precieux pain,
888 Quar il a quarante jours ou plus
Qu'il ne mangast.

MARIE

Las, il a fain!

GABRIEL

Ouÿ, dame, il est tout vain
Et grandement travallé.

MARY
My gentle friends,
876 You are most welcome!
Pausa.
Alas, where is my son, Jesus?
Do you bring me any news of him?

URIEL
Truly, we do, madam.

MARY
What news?

GABRIEL
Good news.

MARY
880 How so?

GABRIEL
Because
He has shown great valor
Against Satan and all his power,
884 And has sent him away in ruin.

MARY
What else?

GABRIEL
Know, madam, that from on high
We bring him this precious bread,
888 For he has gone forty days or more
Without eating.

MARY
Poor man, he is hungry.

GABRIEL
Yes, madam, he is very weak
And has suffered much pain.

MARIE 16a

892 Mon soupper est apparellé;
Je vouldroie bien, mes amys,
Que ycy fust meinctenent mon filz
Pour soupper en ma conpaignie.

GABRIEL

896 Ballés le nous, vierge Marie;
De bon cueur le luy pourterons.

MARIE

Or tenés doncques, mes mignhons.
Vous me faictes ung grant plaisir;
900 Plus grant ne sçaroie chouysir,
Fors que le veoir, je vous affie.

GABRIEL

Adieu, meistresse!

RAPHAEL

Adieu, m'amye!

URIEL

Marie, a Dieu vous conmant!

Tunc vadant angelli supra montem ubi est Jhesus.

MARIE

904 A Dieu vous conmant! Tout meinctenent
Avec mon filz je vouldroye estre.
De joye mon cueur feroit croistre
Et eslever jusques es cieulx.
908 Mes quel pleisir aroient mes yeulx!
Hee, Dieu, quant je pansse se bien,
Il me semble que je le tien,
Tant suis en amours eslevee.
912 Hee, Jhesus, ma doulce brassee,
Et que ne vous tiens je ycy?
Advanssés vous, mon doulx amy;

MARY

892 My supper is ready;
I wish, my friends,
That my son could be here now
To sup in my company!

GABRIEL

896 Give it to us, Mary Virgin;
Gladly will we take it to him.

MARY

Take it, then, my dear ones.
You do me great pleasure;
900 A greater could I not hope for,
Unless it were to see him, I swear to you.

GABRIEL

Farewell, madam!

RAPHAEL

Farewell, beloved one!

URIEL

Farewell, Mary!

Then let the angels go up to the mountain where Jesus is.

MARY

904 Farewell. I wish I could be
With my son right now.
He would make my heart swell with joy.
And raise it up to the heavens.
908 And what pleasure would he bring to my eyes!
O God, when I think about it,
It seems that I am holding him,
So exalted am I made by my love.
912 O Jesus, my sweet darling,
Why do I not hold you in my arms here?
Come, my sweet love;

Venés a moy que je vous voye.
916 Jhesus m'amour, Jhesus ma joye,
Jhesus le seul bien de mon ame,
Je suis celle pouvrecte famme
Que vous faictes d'amour languir.
920 Conbien que n'ay aultre desir
Que vous veoir, ma seulle esperance,
Puis donc que c'est voustre pleisance
D'alleurs estre, j'en suis joyeuse.

Pausa modica.

JHESUS 16b
924 Las, Dieu, mon pere, si j'eusse
Ung peu du soupper de ma mere
Ou du pain prins en ton repaire,
J'en mangeroie vraiement.

GABRIEL
928 *Valle*, Jhesus, saulveur du firmament!

JHESUS
Avete, mes amys!

GABRIEL
Dieu tout puissant
A toy nous a tramys,
932 Nous conmandant
Que te soyons subgis
Pour toy servir.
Nous avons pris
936 Le soupper de ta mere
Et se pein bis,
Conbien que Dieu le pere
Te peut nourrir.

JHESUS
940 J'ay grant pleisir
Des biens que me pourtés

Come to me that I may see you.
916 Jesus my love, Jesus my joy,
Jesus the pride of my soul,
I am that poor woman
Whom you make languish with love.
920 Although I have no other desire
But to see you, my only hope,
Since it is your will
To be elsewhere, I am content.

Pausa modica.

JESUS
924 Alas, God, my father, if I had
A little of my mother's supper,
Or some bread from her home,
I would eat it, truly.

GABRIEL
928 *Vale*, Jesus, savior of the world!

JESUS
Avete, my friends!

GABRIEL
Almighty God
Has sent us to you,
932 Commanding us
To place ourselves
At your service.
We have brought
936 The meal your mother has made
And also this brown bread,
Although God the Father
Can nourish you.

JESUS
940 I am very glad to receive
The things you bring me,

Ad moy saisir
En mes necessités,
944 Car j'ay grant fain.

GABRIEL
Se sont nouvellectés
Qu'il te falle manger.

JHESUS
Humeines pouvrectés
948 M'ont mys en ce danger.
Car suis humain.

RAPHAEL
Or mange de se pain
Que du ciel t'aportons.

Tunc comedat Jhesus et fiat modica pausa.

URIEL
952 Il est fait sans levain.

GABRIEL
Le soupper vous pourtons
De Marie.

Tunc comedat Jhesus de sena Marie et post dicat.

17a

JHESUS
Que ses mourceaulx sont bons!

GABRIEL
956 Or mengés d'appetit,
Et puis nous en yrons.

JHESUS
J'ay assés de petit
Pour ma vie.

Facta comestione reddit gracias et dicit.

To give to me
In my need,
944 For indeed I am very hungry.

GABRIEL
There is something rare here
For you to eat.

JESUS
Human frailty
948 Has put me in this condition,
For I am human.

RAPHAEL
Now, eat this bread,
Which we bring you from heaven.

Then let Jesus eat, and let there be a modica pausa.

URIEL
952 It is unleavened bread.

GABRIEL
Now we bring you a meal
From Mary.

Then let Jesus eat Mary's supper, and afterwards let him say:

JESUS
How good this tastes!

GABRIEL
956 Now, eat heartily,
And then we shall go.

JESUS
I need only a little,
For sustenance.

Having finished the meal, he gives thanks and says:

960 Dieu qu'en terre m'as mys
Soit loué de ses biens,
Des quieulx il me nourrist.
Or ne veulx je plus riens.
964 Les hommes que sont tiens
Donné m'as, Dieu mon pere,
Car tes biens sont tous miens.
Je t'en rans lye chere.

GABRIEL
968 Or allons a ta mere
Pour bien la resjouÿr.
Nous luy ferons pleisir
Si l'allons visicter.

JHESUS
972 Allons!

GABRIEL
Doncques chanter
Nous fault pour l'amour de Marie.

Tunc vadant angelli ad Mariam cum Jhesu et cantent ea que sequntur in cantu: Beata es Maria.

ANGELLI *cantando*
Glorieuse Marie,
De Dieu pleisant amye,
976 Or faictes chere lye,
Car veez cy voustre vye,
Glorieuse Marie!
Marie, mere de douleur,
980 Mere de grace et d'onneur
Et mere de noustre seigneur,
Vous estes garde du pecheur,
Glorieuse Marie!

984 A toy, glouere, benoit Jhesus, 17b

960 God, who has sent me to earth,
Be praised for his gifts,
With which he has nourished me.
I could not wish for anything more.
964 Mankind, which is yours,
You have given to me, God my father,
For what is yours is mine.
I thank you with all my heart.

GABRIEL
968 Now let us go to your mother,
To gladden her heart.
We shall give her great joy,
If we go to visit her.

JESUS
972 Yes, let us go.

GABRIEL
So let us
Sing, out of our love for Mary.

Then let the angels go to Mary with Jesus and let them sing the words that follow to the tune of the hymn: Beata es Maria.

THE ANGELS *singing*
Blessed Mary,
Beloved of God,
976 Now be merry,
Behold here your life,
Blessed Mary!
Mary, mother of sorrows,
980 Mother of grace and honor,
And mother of our lord,
You are the protector of sinners,
Blessed Mary!

984 All praise to thee, blessed Jesus,

Et a ton pere de la sus!
Avec voustre seint esperit
Vous avés de grace ranplit
988 Glorieuse Marie!

Tunc recedunt angelli ad paradisum et Jhesus ingreditur domum Marie, et Maria loquitur et dicit sequencia verba.

MARIA

Souverein Dieu, quelle mellodie!
Mon cueur en est trestout joyeulx.
A mon Dieu soit la chanterie
992 De vous seinctz anges glorïeux.
Seroit ce point mon amoureux
Qui me vient* ycy veoir? (MS vint)
Se je le puis appercevoir,
996 De tout bien renpliré mes yeulx.
Pausa. Certes, c'est mon filz gracïeulx.
Il fault bien que voyse a luy.

JHESUS

Valete, mere!

MARIE

Hee, mon amy,
1000 Vous soyés le tresbien venu.
Et quoy, m'amour, vous avés heu
Affaire des que ne vous veix?

JHESUS

Ouÿ, mere.

MARIE

Et bien, mon filz,
1004 C'est tousjours pour admeriter.
Il vous fault ung peu repouser,
Quar je sçay qu'estes travallé;
Et quant vous arés sonmellé

And to your father on high!
Through your holy spirit
You have filled with grace
988 Blessed Mary!

Then the angels return to Paradise and Jesus enters Mary's house, and Mary speaks and says the following words.

MARY
Almighty God, what music do I hear!
My heart fills with joy at the sound.
May the singing of your blessed angels
992 Be for the glory of my God.
Could it be that even now my beloved
Is coming here to see me?
If only I can see him,
996 My eyes will be filled with all good.
It is, it is my blessed son!
I must go to him!

JESUS
Valete, mother!

MARY
Oh, my beloved,
1000 You are most welcome.
Tell me, my love, have you done
Some business since I last saw you?

JESUS
Yes, mother.

MARY
Well, my son,
1004 You are always earning glory.
You must rest for a while,
For I know that you are weary;
And when you have slumbered

1008 Et dormy ung peu sur ce banc,
Vous arés voustre entendement
Mieulx a voustre ayse, mon amy.

JHESUS
Ma mere, je vous rans mercy.
1012 Volantiers je prandré se bien!

MARIA
Pour ce jour ne feron plus riens!
A Dieu soyons trestous!

Explicit.

Deo gracias.

1008 And slept a bit on this bench,
Your mind will be much refreshed,
My beloved.

JESUS
I thank you, mother,
1012 Gladly shall I accept what you offer.

MARY
We shall do no more work today!
May we all be in God's hands!

The End.

Deo gracias.

Explanatory Notes

The Characters

SAMUEL: the name appears in the apocryphal *Acts of Pilate*, where Samuel is named, along with Zeras, Jacob, Phineas, and Lazarus, as being among the twelve Jewish councillors, secret adherents of Jesus, who defended Jesus before Pilate. See Introduction, 3.3.2. On Scribe B's "canonization" of this character, see 1.2.3, note 8.

ANDREW: i.e., Saint Andrew. See John 1 : 35–40; Luke 6 : 13.

NATHANAEL: mentioned as a disciple of John the Baptist in John 1 : 45–51.

NASON: the name comes from the *Passion d'Auvergne*, where Nason is, as here, a converted Pharisee who becomes a follower of John the Baptist. He is given the same role in the *Passion de Semur*. In the Jean Michel *Passion*, on the other hand, as well as in the Mons *Passion* of 1501, the name is given to a Pharisee sent by Herod to interrogate John the Baptist.

JOSEPH OF ARIMATHAEA: called a "disciple" of Jesus in Matthew 27 : 58 and John 19 : 38. In the Gospels he appears only after the Crucifixion.

JACOB: see under Samuel, above.

ZERAS: see under Samuel, above.

NICODEMUS: see John 3 : 1–9, 19 : 39.

PHINEAS: see under Samuel, above.

LAZAY: i.e., Lazarus. See under Samuel, above. Not to be confused with the biblical Lazarus, commonly called "Le Lazare" or "Le Ladre" in French.

HEROD: Herod Antipas, son of Herod the Great.

MALIFFERAS: the name means "bearer of evil." See Introduction, 2.1.4 and 3.6.2.

CAIAPHAS, ANNAS: Caiaphas was Annas's son-in-law and had succeeded him as High Priest at the time of Jesus's ministry (Luke 3 : 2). By tradition in medieval literature and drama, the two are treated as contemporaries and co-equals.

NATORT: from the *Passion d'Auvergne*, where the name is spelled "Nachor." In Gréban's *Passion* "Nachor" is a Sadducee; in Michel's *Passion*, a scribe.

BERITH: from the *Passion d'Auvergne*, where the name is spelled "Beric." The name is derived from Jacobus de Voragine's *Legenda aurea* (see p. 479 in the Ryan and Ripperger translation). In both Gréban and Michel it is used as the name of a devil.

LUCIFER: see Isaiah 14 : 12.

SATAN: see Matthew 4 : 10.

BEELZEBUB: in 2 Kings 1 : 2, a Philistine god; in Matthew 10 : 25, Mark 3 : 22, and Luke 11 : 15–19, the Prince of Demons.

ASHTORETH: in Judges 10 : 6 and in 1 Kings 11 : 5 a Canaanite goddess. Listed as a devil in the *Legenda aurea* (p. 479).

ASMO: probably a diminutive of Asmodée or Asmodeus, a demon in the Book of Tobit 3 : 17. The diminutive form also occurs in the *Passion d'Auvergne*.

The Text

Incipit: quantité: ambiguous; it may mean the contents of the play, or the number of characters; probably the former.

premier dimanche: probably synonymous with *première journée;* see Introduction, 2.1.2.

tres coronas: i.e., a triple crown or papal tiara.

(*sceptrum*): the manuscript gives a drawing of a sceptre rather than the word itself.

sanctus Johannis . . . pillis chamelli: the description copies Matthew 3 : 4.

1: The first lines show the traditional beginning of a *mystère*—an effort to silence the audience, here with some music. (See Carnahan, *The Prologue in the Old French Mysteries.*)

2: *rondel.* A *rondel* is a part-song, similar to a round, in which two or three melodies are sung simultaneously by as many voices, each voice singing each melody in turn. Originally the *rondel* was used only for sacred texts. In the later Middle Ages, however, the word became synonymous with *rondeau*, a strophic song of four lines in which the second and fourth lines are refrains, and of which the text might be either secular or sacred. As *rondeau* is the more familiar modern word, it has been used in the translation. (See Reese, *Music in the Middle Ages.*)

2 S.D.: *cantus comunis.* The context suggests that the *rondel* is sung by the whole choir of angels, *conpaignons* in line 1 presumably referring to Raphael's fellow-angels. The term *comunis* possibly refers to the audience as well, in which case we should have to take *conpaignons* as also including the audience. In 868 S.D., however, the same phrase, *cantu comuni*, clearly refers only to the angels.

3: *Concinamus nato Emanuel.* The first line of what appears to be a hymn—"Let us sing to the son, Emmanuel." We have not been able to trace such a hymn.

6: *Zacarie.* Luke 1 : 5–25.

13–16: Mark 1 : 4–6.

27–28 : Matthew 3 : 16–7.

31–37: Ludolphus, following St. John Chrysostom, describes the Baptism as the first public manifestation of the Trinity (see *Vita Jesu Christi*, ed. L. M. Rigollet, chap. 21.)

61: The beginning of "Scene 2," introducing Samuel and the other three disciples, occurred in a leaf or leaves now missing from the manuscript. See Introduction, 1.2.3 and 2.1.3. The source of this scene is Matthew 3 : 5–6. The scene is paralleled in the *Passion de Semur*, lines 3429–62.

66 S.D.: *Pausa cum silete.* For the meaning of these terms see Introduction, 2.4.2.

71–78: These lines constitute a *triolet*, a form of *rondeau* frequently used in *mystères*, sometimes accompanied by music. See Jean Michel's so-called *rondeaux dramatiques*, and above, 5.2.5(1).

101: The beginning of "Scene 3." The visit of some Pharisees to John is suggested by Matthew 3 : 7.

106: *Hellias.* 1 Kings 17 : 1–2 Kings 2 : 12.

108: *Ysayas.* Isaiah, passim; Ecclesiastes 48 : 23–24.
111: *papias.* The context clearly gives this word the sense of paper, but the form of the word is very unusual, largely influenced no doubt by the complex and demanding rhymes in *-ias* on alternate lines from 105 to 126.
112: *estutier.* Again an unusual spelling; normally *estudier.*
113: *Geremias.* See Book of Jeremiah.
116: *Hollofernes.* Judith 2 : 4. *Goliath.* 1 Samuel 17 : 1–51.
118 : Herodias. Luke 3 : 19.
121: "*Parate vias.*" "Prepare the way"—the first words of John's sermon as reported by Luke 3 : 4. This and the following sermon have been lost from the manuscript after line 60.
122: "*Faictes trestous penictence.*" The first words of John's sermon reported by Matthew 3 : 2.
123: *Thobias.* See Book of Tobias (or Tobit).
130: *Ego sum vox clamantis.* "I am the voice crying [in the wilderness]." Matthew 3 : 3, Mark 1 : 3, Luke 3 : 4, John 1 : 23, quoting Isaiah 40 : 3.
146: Matthew 3 : 7.
156: Matthew 3 : 10.
162–65: Luke 3 : 10–11.
166–72: Luke 3 : 12–14.
190 S.D.: A good example of the simultaneous action used in the staging of the play. See Introduction, 2.3.
202: *admeriter.* The sense here, and at line 1004, is slightly different from the usual dictionary translation of *mériter.* Both examples seem to have a transitive meaning: "to bring merit or honor to other people."
218–26: Ludolphus, following Chrysostom, writes that Jesus was baptized, not to cleanse himself of sin, but to purify the waters of baptism through his own innocence, so that they might wash away the sins of man. (See *Vita Jesu Christi*, ed. Rigollet, chap. 21.)
232 S.D.: *ponendo aquam supra eos.* Emile Mâle notes that pictorial representations of the Baptism down to the twelfth century showed Jesus and the disciples immersed in the river Jordan, reflecting liturgical practice at a time when only adults were baptized. As infant baptism grew commoner,

baptism by immersion was replaced by baptism by "infusion," usually accomplished by holding a vial of water over the initiate's head. (*Les saints*, p. 26.) See also Leonel L. Mitchell, *Baptismal Anointing* (London, 1966).

233 S.D.: *Tunc judicamur*. This addition of Scribe B's appears to be a line of liturgical significance related to the baptism of John's disciples, possibly the first line of a hymn. We have been unable to trace its origin.

235: The beginning of "Scene 4." The scene is based on the *Meditationes Vitae Christi* of Pseudo-Bonaventure. Jesus's farewell to Mary is also described by Ludolphus and dramatized by Gréban (lines 10247–78) and Michel (1801–994).

249: *brassee*. The normal meaning of this word, arm's length or armful, has been extended to something one can embrace through love; hence, darling.

253: *muer lieu*. This expression has a staging sense as well as a more general meaning. The *lieu* was a technical term for an area of the stage associated with a particular place or character, without being a fully constructed "mansion."

259–70: Mary's prayer here "covers" Jesus's journey to John the Baptist. For the staging principle, see Introduction, 2.2.1.

277–86: Matthew 3 : 13–6.

278: *Baptiser*. This line, which falls outside the normal system of versification, upsets the regular rhythm, and thus draws attention to what is the crucial subject of this episode, the baptism of Jesus by John.

290 S.D.: The stage direction in brackets, added by Scribe B, calls for the descent of the dove 20 lines before Scribe A envisaged it. See 1.2.3 above.

295–96: Ludolphus writes that the Baptism constituted Christ's establishment of His universal church and His invitation to all men to be purified through it (chap. 21).

298: *circunsision ara fin*. Ludolphus, following Chrysostom, comments that the Baptism of Christ abolished the "Jewish baptism," i.e., circumcision, just as later His celebration of the Passover would abolish the old rite and institute a new sacrament (chap. 21).

300 S.D.: *anges*. The scriptural accounts of the Baptism make

no mention of angels being present. The angels were supplied by Chrysostom and most later commentators on the scene. Their function, according to Ludolphus, is to call men to a life in heaven, for which they are now eligible (chap. 21).

305: *cresme.* "Cream;" but perhaps also a pun on *chresme*, "chrism" or holy oil used in the baptismal service.

311–26: The music here "covers" the descent of the angels from the Heaven scaffold and their movement across the playing-area.

318 S.D.: *copula.* The word clearly means "stanza" or "verse" here, although this is not its usual meaning. Cf. Provençal *cobla.*

340: The Scriptures do not record the baptism of John by Jesus. It was inferred, however, by the early Church Fathers, notably by Chrysostom in his *Homily 12 on Matthew.* (See Hennecke, ed., *New Testament Apocrypha*, 2 : 38 ff.)

344 S.D.: The actual song sung by the angels as they return to Paradise is not given. It is presumably a reprise of the song given in lines 311–26.

346: *m'amye.* 2 Corinthians 11 : 2.

358–60: Baptism in the name of the Trinity reflects medieval liturgical practice rather than scriptural fact. See Woolf, *The English Mystery Plays*, p. 218.

361–68: Another *rondeau dramatique;* see note on 71–78.

368 S.D.: *recedens.* I.e., towards the Desert. Jesus speaks his monologue while walking from the Jordan to the Desert, which he reaches at line 389.

403: The beginning of "Scene 5." The author here models Herod Antipas's consultation with the High Priests about John on the earlier Herod Agrippa's consultation with his "chief priests and scribes" about the birth of Jesus (Matthew 2 : 4). The New Testament makes no connection between John and Annas and Caiaphas; the author here identifies the latter with "the Jews" who send "priests and Levites from Jerusalem" to interrogate John (John 1 : 19).

During this scene Jesus remains in view, in the Desert.

419–20: *rante . . . Sesar.* An allusion to Luke 2 : 1—another indication that the author has "confused" the events surrounding the Baptism with those at the birth of Christ.

442–44: Deuteronomy 18 : 15.

446: Malachi 4 : 5–6; Matthew 11 : 9–10; Luke 1 : 17.

447–50: Genesis 49 : 10–12.

449–50: The syntax of these lines is more characteristic of Latin than of French.

454: *Jacaret*. The name probably read *Zacarie* in the original version of the play. See line 6, and 5.3 above.

483: The beginning of "Scene 6." The biblical source of the interrogation of John is John 1 : 19–28. The scene is dramatized by both Gréban (10171–246) and Michel (1711–800); the *Passion de Semur* shows only the arrest of John by Beric and Nachor (3629–4126).

483–90: John's brief sermon "covers" the journey of Malifferas and his companions from the Temple to the Jordan.

489–90: A paraphrase of John 3 : 30.

537–45: This dialgogue is spoken during the return journey of Malifferas and his companions to the Temple.

545: The soldiers, messengers, and *tyrans* (torturers) in *mystères* were traditionally given to bouts of drinking and other forms of comic relief. There may well have been an unwritten interlude at this point. The characters here show their descent from the *miles gloriosus* of classical comedy.

563–64: The lines suggest that a future scene, on another day of the play, was to have included the arrest of John and his appearance before Herod. See Introduction, 2.1.5.

565. The beginning of "Scene 7." The Council in Hell was a traditional addition to the scriptural narrative in both English and continental Passion plays. It functions as a prologue to the Temptation and cannot be traced to any single literary or theological source. Other instances of the scene in French drama include *Semur* (4127–236), Gréban (10417–529), and Michel (2196–366).

The *diablerie* here was probably accompanied by much infernal music, banging of drums, smoke and flames, intended to invoke laughter. The scene contains a number of complex verse forms: in addition to the standard octosyllabic couplets, there are two *rondeaux dramatiques* (662–69, 682–89), and three other different stanza forms. See above, 5.2.

The stage direction *Pausa cum cilete* is the first major break in the action for Scribe A (see 1.2.3 above). John the Baptist's role is over, and the Temptation episode begins.

569–70: *Enfer . . . Cerberus.* Both of these names appear, in the context, to be synonyms for Lucifer. In Gréban and Michel, however, "Enfer" is the name of a devil, as "Cerberus" appears to be at line 835 below.

578–79: The sense is a bit obscure here. The lines appear to refer to lines 278–82, where John is at first reluctant to baptize Jesus but soon agrees to do so, thus enabling Jesus to begin his work of sanctifying the human race (293).

584: *enfer.* Here, Hell itself, and in particular Hell-Mouth, the dragon's jaws serving as the entrance to Hell. The speech may, however, be addressed to Lucifer, as at 569 and 628 below.

588: *eux nians.* One of the few passages where the reading of the manuscript is unclear. Presumably the sense is that if Lucifer hesitates and shows fear at the sight of Jesus, he will cause his fellow devils to reject him as their leader.

636: Genesis 4 : 8.

637–39 : 2 Samuel 11 : 15–7.

640: 2 Samuel 13 : 1–29.

641: 2 Samuel 20 : 8–10.

642–43: Judges 9 : 1–5.

672: *lectres procuratoueres.* For the sources of the judicial terminology used in this passage, see Roy, *Le mystère de la Passion en France*, pp. 361, 411–14.

698: *Accopt.* Exclamation expressing urgency.

700: The beginning of "Scene 8." The biblical sources for the Temptation in the Wilderness are Matthew 4 : 1–11 and Luke 4 : 1–13. The order of the three temptations here follows that of Matthew rather than that of Luke, who places the temptation on the Temple last.

700–25: Jesus's prayer covers the journey of Satan and Asmo to the Desert.

700 S.D.: *in veste heremite.* On Satan's disguise, see Ellinger, "Uber den Teufel als Monch."

737–38: Deuteronomy 8 : 3.

746 S.D.: *portat*. In the Michel *Passion* this is accomplished by Satan placing Jesus on his shoulders, whereupon the two are lifted to the top of the structure by a "contrepoys."

754 S.D.: *sacerdotis*. The Devil was frequently represented in medieval art as wearing a theologian's hood for the Temptation on the Temple. An example is the painting of the scene by Lucas van Leyden. Ludolphus, quoting St. Bernard, explains that Satan chose the Temple as the appropriate site for a temptation to vainglory because it was the "seat of the doctors" (chap. 21). Satan's reference to a "hood" (*hocte*) at 794 also suggests this costuming.

759, 768: Psalms 91 : 11–2.

774: Deuteronomy 6 : 16.

782: *huis*. The "gate" leads to a flight of steps, as explained in Ludolphus: "Comme Jésus-Christ pouvait descendre du pinacle autrement que par un miracle, puisqu'il y avait de larges degrés, il répondit alors 'Vous ne tenterez pas' . . ." (chap. 22 in the translation of the *Vita* by M. P. Augustin).
The elliptical grammar of our text is clarified by Ludolphus's original Latin: "Ego autem homo sum, et aliter possum descendere, quam per jactantiam me praecipitare" (Rigollet ed., 1 : 200). The theological point is that Jesus refuses to misuse his divine power for magical purposes and instead returns to the ground in a natural human way.

787–97: The devils here speak in a new stanza-structure; see note to 565.

811: A comic variation on the usually more exotic list of Satan's domains. Michel gives "Arrabe, Tarsse, Asye, Affrique,/Egipte, Calde, Babilonne" (3060–62).

829–44: Yet another new verse-form; see Introduction, 5.2.

835: *dant Serberus*. Possibly the teeth of Hell-Mouth itself, or those of a doglike devil. On the history of Cerberus in medieval demonology, see Owen, *The Vision of Hell*, pp. 143–44, 264–65.

839: *Targnanam*. Unidentified.

844: *Galgatin*. Unidentified.

844 S.D.: *Pausa cum cilete*. The second major break in the action for Scribe A. The Temptation episode is over, and the scene

of the angels and Mary ministering to Jesus after his fasting is to follow, as a *coda* to the first day.

845: The beginning of "Scene 9." The only hint for this scene in the Scriptures is Matthew's report that after the Temptation "angels came and ministered unto him" (4 : 11). The principal source is the *Meditationes vitae Christi*, chap. 17. Some details come, however, from the derivative but slightly different account in Ludolphus, chap. 22. The scene is either missing or highly truncated in other Passion plays of the period. See Introduction, 3.5.2.

The first part of the scene is written in verse forms other than the neutral octosyllabic couplet. The angels also sing yet another *rondeau dramatique*.

868 S.D.: *cantu comuni*. A song for all the angels, not just Gabriel, Uriel, and Raphael. It covers their descent to Mary's house.

904–23: Mary's prayer covers the journey of the angels to the Mountain, where Jesus has remained after the abortive Temptation by Satan and Asmo.

928: *Valle*. I.e., *vale*, "hail."

933: *subgis*. The normal form, *sujet/subject*, is altered here, perhaps because of the demands of a difficult rhyme scheme.

951 S.D. *fiat modica pausa*. For details of the silent tableau that takes place here, see Introduction, 3.5.3.

973 S.D.: *Beata es Maria:* "Blessed art thou, Mary." The French verses that follow are fitted to the tune of this Latin hymn. For the original Latin text, see *Analecta Hymnica Medii Aevi*, ed. G. M. Dreves (New York, 1961), 20 : 182.

974–96: The angels' song to Mary covers their journey back from the Mountain with Jesus to Mary's house. The angels leave Jesus outside the house (she hears their *mellodie* at 989), and go back up to Paradise. Mary's brief monologue allows Jesus time to enter the house.

1013–14: This speech is probably addressed to the audience.

1014 S.D.: *Deo gracias*. "Thanks be to God." The Scribe's pious note, not a line of dialogue.

Bibliography

Beaulieux, C. *Histoire de l'orthographe française*. Paris, 1927.

Bonaventure [Pseudo-Bonaventure]. *Meditationes Vitae Christi*. Translated by W. H. Hutchings. London, 1881.

Bossuat, A. "Une représentation de la Passion à Montferrand en 1477." *Bibliothèque d'humanisme et Renaissance* 5 : 326–45.

Briquet, C. M. *Les Filigranes*. Jubilee edition. Edited by A. Stevenson. Amsterdam, 1968.

Brown, H. M. *Music in the French Secular Theatre, 1400–1550*. Cambridge, Mass., 1963.

Brunot, F. *Histoire de la langue française*. Vol. 2. Paris, 1924.

Carnahan, D. *The Prologue in the Old French Mysteries*. New Haven, 1905.

Chocheyras, J. *Le théâtre religieux en Savoie au XVIe siècle*. Geneva, 1971.

Ellinger, G. "Uber den Teufel als Monch." *Zeitschrift für Vergleichende Literatur-Geschichte*, n.s. 1, 174–81.

Fouquet, J. *The Hours of Etienne Chevalier*. Edited by Cl. Schaefer. New York, 1971.

Frank, G. *The Medieval French Drama*. Oxford, 1954.

Gascoigne, B. *World Theatre: An Illustrated History*. London, 1968.

Hennecke, Edgar and Schneemelcher, Wilhelm, eds. *New Testament Apocrypha*. Translated by R. M. Wilson. 2 vols. London, 1963.

Greban, A. *Mystère de la Passion*. Edited by O. Jodogne. Brussels, 1965.

James, M., ed. *The Apocryphal New Testament*. Oxford, 1953.

Jeanroy, A. "Sur quelques sources des mystères de la Passion." *Romania* 35 : 365–78.

Jerome. *The Homilies of Saint Jerome.* Translated by Sister M. L. Ewald. 2 vols. *Fathers of the Church,* vols. 48, 57. Washington D.C., 1966.

Jodogne, O. "La structure des mystères français." *Revue belge de philologie et histoire* 42 : 827–42.

Konigson, E. *La représentation d'un mystère de la Passion à Valenciennes en 1547.* Paris, 1969.

Lieftinck, G. I. *Manuscrits datés conservés dans les Pays-Bas.* Amsterdam, 1964.

Lote, G. *Histoire du vers français.* Paris, 1955.

Ludolphus de Saxonia. *Vita Iesu Christi.* Translated by M. P. Augustin. 4 vols. Paris, 1864.

———. *Vita Jesu Christi.* Edited by L. M. Rigollet. 2 vols. Paris and Brussels, 1878.

Male, E. *L'art religieux de la fin du Moyen Age en France.* Paris, 1931.

———. *Les saints: Compagnons du Christ.* Paris, 1958.

Michel, J. *Le mystère de la Passion.* Edited by O. Jodogne, Gembloux, 1959.

Owen, D. D. R. *The Vision of Hell.* Edinburgh, 1970.

Passion de Semur. Edited by E. Roy (1903–04).

Petit de Julleville, L. *Les mystères.* 2 vols. Paris, 1880.

Picot, E. "Fragments inédits de mystères de la Passion." *Romania* 19 (1890) : 26–82.

Pope, M. *From Latin to Modern French.* Manchester, 1934.

Prou, M. *Recueil de fac-similés.* Paris, 1904.

Reese, Gustave. *Music in the Middle Ages.* New York, 1940.

Roy, E. *Le mystère de la Passion en France.* 2 vols. Paris and Dijon. (*Revue Bourgignonne* 13–14). 1903–04.

Runnalls, G., ed. *Le mystère de la Passion Nostre Seigneur.* Geneva, 1974.

———. "The Linguistic Dating of Middle French Texts." *Modern Language Review* 71 (1976) : 757–65.

Rydberg, G. *Geschichte des französischen e.* Uppsala, 1898.

Thurot, C. *De la prononciation française depuis le commencement du XVIe siècle.* Paris, 1881.

Voragine, J. *Legenda aurea.* Translated by G. Ryan and H. Ripperger. New York, 1941.
Woolf, R. *The English Mystery Plays.* Berkeley and Los Angeles, 1972.